Wolfdogs A-Z

Behavior, Training & More

Nicole Wilde

Wolfdogs A-Z: Behavior, Training & More

ISBN 0-9667726-1-X

Photos on the following pages were taken by Monty Sloan:
53, 55, 67, 83, 160, 165, 170, 186, 199, 202, 238

Due to legal issues involving wolfdogs, no other specific photo
credits are given. This is to protect the photographers and their animals.
Thank you all, you know who you are.

Diagram p. 65: Joell Severns
Cover photo: Nicole Wilde
Back cover photo: Leslie Bockian

ACKNOWLEDGEMENTS

I would like to thank the following people:

Dr. Ian Dunbar, without whose insight, encouragement and friendship this book would not have come to be. If canines could speak, millions would thank Dr. Dunbar for bringing positive, gentle training to the forefront and making it the standard for the future.

Monty Sloan, for his input, feedback and for the usual amazing photographs. Monty, you're still the world's best wolf-pretzler!

Laura Bourhenne, a good friend and great trainer, for always being willing to share her knowledge and resources, and for all those long lunches discussing "dog stuff."

Maryellen Cecelia Hankele for her feedback, friendship, and relentless encouragement.

Gudrun Dunn, for her excellent written and photographic contributions; Paul Ferrari, for bravely sharing his experience of Winter Wolf Syndrome; Jill Porter, for the Bunny Sit info, photographs and the great Fuschia Frisbee story; Joell Severns, for the wonderful suggestions on enrichment, and her friendship; Dr. Diane Delbridge, for the absolutely awesome veterinary chapter; Christine Burkett, for the bottle-feeding recipe; Barbara, Jacque and especially Brett at Candy Kitchen for letting me visit and photograph their wolfdogs; Sharon, Bill and Kobuk Voden for being such great models; and Glenn Bullock and Michele Tarvan for friendship and support during the writing of this book.

For photographic/other contributions: Diane Horne, Ann Dresselhaus, Beth Palmer, and my wonderful friends, Michelle and Bruce Silmon.

And last but not least, thanks to my amazing husband for being so supportive and as usual, putting up with all the "crazy wolf stuff."

Although in 1993 the Smithsonian reclassified dogs as a subspecies of wolf based on genetic studies conducted by Dr. Robert Wayne, such does not negate the use of the term "hybrid," nor the scientific validity of its use. However, due to the negative connotations associated with the term "wolf hybrid" in the media and by certain factions which strive to make it illegal to own an animal with recent wolf ancestry, I have chosen to use the term "wolfdog" henceforth in this book.

Reference is made throughout this book to content, i.e. "a low content wolfdog." This refers to approximately how much wolf is in the wolfdog mix. For our purposes, "low content" is roughly up to 35% wolf; "mid-content" falls between 36-74% and "high content," 75% and up.

Note: "98%" is an expression used by many wolfdog owners to denote a pure wolf, when saying "pure wolf" is likely to invite questions of legality.

Wolfdogs are referred to herein in the male gender. This does not imply any gender bias, but is simply for ease of reading.

Table of Contents

Table of Contents

Foreword

My first book, *Living with Wolfdogs*, offered a realistic view of what sharing one's life with these controversial companions is like. It included pros and cons, day-to-day issues, and plenty of how-to (and how-not-to!) advice. Since its publication, many have written to say that the information helped them to decide whether or not to get a wolfdog. For others, it made the difference in being able to keep their beloved companion, whether by learning how to build proper containment, establish better leadership, or being able to bond with fearful, rescued wolfdogs. (The latter really warmed my heart.) Along with all this wonderful feedback came a flood of questions regarding behavior and training. It became obvious that these topics needed to be addressed.

Thanks to these requests for further information, along with some well-intentioned pestering by friends (and you know who you are), this second book took shape. It covers behavioral issues in detail, and provides step-by-step training techniques that are fun, effective and easy to follow. A few of the chapters are not behavior or training related, but are important enough to warrant inclusion, such as the sections on feeding raw foods and on veterinary care.

The information presented herein was gathered through years of hands-on training, reading, attending seminars, networking with other trainers, and by just being a plain ol' Woof Mom. The techniques and suggestions offered have certainly helped me, and I sincerely hope they will help you to enhance your relationship with your own four-legged companions. Just remember, no matter what the training or behavior modification method, the most important ingredients for success are patience, consistency and kindness. Oh yes, and lots of tummyrubs!

Wolfdogs A-Z

Though you may read this book straight through, it is formatted conveniently so that each chapter stands on its own for quick reference. Many chapters will refer you to other sections which contain more information on that particular subject. So jump in!

Howls,
Nicole Wilde

Note: Wolfdogs are not the perfect pet for the average person. Though loving, intelligent, wonderful companions, they take a lot more time, effort and patience than the average doggie-dog. For the purposes of this book, I am assuming that you already share your life with a wolfdog. If not, and you are trying to decide whether this is the companion for you, please refer to Living with Wolfdogs *and make a careful, considered decision.*

Alpha

Most wolf packs have an "alpha pair." This male/female dynamic duo mate, produce pups and generally lead the pack. Every pack has a social structure, or hierarchy, which includes all members. Beta is second in rank to alpha, with ranks descending from there all the way down to omega, the lowest. However, this pecking order is not written in stone and may change with circumstance or over time.

Pack order is maintained through communication and cooperation. Subordinate wolves may be reprimanded by higher-ranking members through growls, hard stares and even muzzle pins (putting one's teeth over another's muzzle). Smart subordinates roll over and say "Sorry! Didn't mean it!" and peace is restored to the pack. Interestingly, it is usually middle-ranking wolves rather than the alpha who start squabbles. Alphas, though indisputably in charge, are not bullies; they have nothing to prove. Good alphas settle disagreements quickly with just as much force as is necessary, then move on.

The concept of "being alpha" is important to wolfdog owners. It is also often misunderstood:

"My wolfdog jumps on me. He's trying to be alpha."
"My pup nips at my hands. She wouldn't do that if she understood I'm the boss."
"I tried to get him into the car; he bit me! What nerve!"

What's really going on in these situations? The first wolfdog may have simply been trying to get his owner's attention, and hasn't yet been taught a better way. The second is just a pup, and is

1

most likely playing in what she thinks is an acceptable manner. The third wolfdog is more than likely biting out of fear, rather than from any need to prove dominance. Though any of these wolfdogs might coincidentally have a dominant, pushy, alpha-type temperament, none of the given situations are a clear-cut indication that this is the case.

Leader of the Pack

Something gets lost in the translation from wolf packs to wolfdog-human family units. Some owners (and I use the term loosely, as most are owned *by* these animals) feel that we as humans should play the role of the alpha wolf in every way, relating to our four-footed companions as though we were another wolf. Heck, if that were the case, when a pup licked at our mouth, we'd regurgitate food for them. No thanks!

Of course it's important that your wolfdog look up to you and respect you as leader. In fact, canines who perceive that top spot to be up for grabs may try to fill it themselves. And yes, your wolfdog should feel secure that the alpha (yep, that's you) can handle any situation that comes along. But even in a wolf pack, the alpha is not a total dictator.

Alphas do not, as is commonly thought, *always* eat first, lead the hunt, or stand on the highest point of terrain looking down upon all others. Though one wolf in the pack is certainly deferred to above all the rest, others may appear to be "top dog" temporarily in certain situations. I've watched many an alpha wolf roll on his back when playing with a lower-ranking pack member. The lower-ranking wolf did *not* suddenly send out for champagne, thinking he'd gotten a promotion; and the alpha was obviously not worried about losing his standing. Good alphas, as we should strive to be, communicate clearly and are wise yet playful, kind and fair. They know when to be benevolent and when to enforce pack order. Many people are quick to jump to the conclusion that their wolfdog has a "dominance problem." It may well be that their wolfdog *does* have a strong opinion about who should be in charge. Unfortunately, the human solution to this problem is often to "teach him who's boss" through methods like scruff shakes or alpha rolls. (The most common alpha roll entails rolling the wolfdog on his back and standing over, growling at and/or holding him there until he submits by laying still, looking away or urinating.) These methods are unnecessary and can be downright dangerous to the human attempting them.

Aggression begets aggression. Memorize that phrase—it could save your life. Many canines who have been corrected with physical violence respond by becoming more violent themselves. This can and has resulted in severe injury to owners. Even if the reaction is not immediate, behavior problems can surface later as a result. Besides, you love your wolfdog and want him to respect you, not fear you!

There are ways to clear up your wolfdog's confusion about his place in the pack without using physical force. On the following pages you will find an outline for a Leadership Program. Ideally, it should be started when your wolfdog is a pup. If you have taken in an adult wolfdog, introduce these concepts gradually, taking into account your particular wolfdog's temperament. Please understand that these suggestions do not need to be followed to the letter by all wolfdog owners. For example, if your wolfdog does not show pushy, dominant tendencies, by all means, allow him up on the couch to cuddle if that's your preference. But for a wolfdog who already shows signs of wanting to run the show, follow the program as closely as possible.

Wolfdogs A-Z

Leadership Program

The main thing to remember about being alpha is that *The Leader Controls the Resources.* In your house, the resources include food, water, toys, treats, access to furniture, access to physical space, affection, and anything else your wolfdog finds valuable. Remember, *All Good Things Come From The Leader.*

1. **Food** Food is the number one resource to any canine, as it literally means life or death. Knowing that, do you want your wolfdog to believe that this invaluable resource comes from you, the leader, or that round magical thing on the floor?

Free-feeding means leaving food down at all times. Don't do it. Besides leadership issues, other good reasons for not free-feeding include ease of housebreaking (you need to know when food's going in to know when it's coming out) and health reasons (a missed meal can alert you to illness). Feed twice daily. Let your wolfdog earn his meal by sitting before you put the dish down. If he doesn't finish his meal in ten minutes, pick it up and put the food away.

If you are switching from free to twice-daily feedings, you may find that at the first few feedings, your wolfdog will only take a few nibbles. That's okay. Take the rest away and don't feel guilty. At the next meal, serve half the normal amount. No canine will starve itself; he *will* eventually eat. Don't under any circumstances get into the habit of adding something yummy to your wolfdog's food if he doesn't eat immediately. If you do this, congratulate your wolfdog. He has trained you well! For especially dominant wolfdogs or those who display guarding behavior (see *Guarding*), pick food bowls up after each meal, as you don't want to give him an object to guard.

4

With especially dominant wolfdogs, feed meals by hand for at least a week. (Use caution and your best judgment. Don't hand-feed raw foods if your wolfdog is too grabby with them, and never hand-feed anything to a flat-out aggressive or unfamiliar animal.) Hand-feeding is a very direct way of showing your wolfdog that the most valuable resource there is, the one that literally means life and death, comes from you. You might be surprised by the change this simple act can make in your wolfdog's perception of who's in charge.

2. **Toys** Don't leave toys strewn all over the house. When *you* decide, bring out a toy and engage your companion in play. By playing with him rather than leaving the toy with him, not only are you the Keeper of All Good Things, you are also the Source of Fun! Keeping toys picked up also prevents fighting between canines, and does not allow your wolfdog to guard toys in-between

play sessions. After all, they're not his, they're yours. When playtime is over, say "All done!" and put the toy away.

3. **Furniture** Some people allow their wolfdogs to sleep in bed with them. Others love to snuggle on the couch with their furry friends. Neither of these practices are a problem *as long as your wolfdog has no dominance issues.* If you do allow him up on beds or furniture, be sure he understands a command such as "Get down" so that when you don't want him up there, he understands and respects your wishes. For pushy wolfdogs (i.e. those who snarl "I don't think so" when asked to remove themselves), the bed, couch and anywhere higher than ground level should be off-limits. Those are *your* places. If you are hanging out at floor level with a pushy, dominant-type woofer, do not allow him to lie on or hover over you, even in play.

4. **Play** Playing with your wolfdog is a wonderful thing, and should be done on a daily basis. However, certain types of play can lead to problems. Many people (men in particular) love to wrestle with puppies. They think it's cute—and it is—until the wolfdog matures into a furry Hulk Hogan. Since he's been taught that wrestling is okay and even encouraged, the now-120-pound, heavyweight champion tries out his moves on new opponents. The thing is, parents tend to frown upon a wolfdog trying to engage their five year old child in a wrestling match, friendly or not. *Don't wrestle!* See *Enrichment* for appropriate games.

Tug-of-war has long been thought (those pesky "old wives" again) to cause aggression. Properly played, it doesn't. What does typically happen is, the wolfdog picks up the tug toy (which has been left out, tsk, tsk) and brings it to their person. A tug match ensues. (See how well he's trained you?) Sometimes the wolfdog wins, sometimes the person wins. Things get exciting. The wolfdog gets wound up, and may nip a finger or two while grabbing for the toy... Tug encourages dogs to use their mouths. It also teaches them (if played improperly) that taking things from the leader is possible. Though *there is no scientific evidence that playing tug leads to dominance problems*, for wolfdogs who are already pushy or extremely mouthy, for now, pick a different game. For all others, follow these rules:

Proper Tug-of-Woof

First, be sure your wolfdog absolutely responds to the cue, "Leave It." (If not, see *"Off" (or "Leave It")* and train that first.)

1. Bring out the tug toy (usually a long, thick braided rope) and say, "Wanna play?"
2. Present the toy, saying, "Take it." (Use verbal cues 1 and 2 each time you bring out the toy.)
3. Allow your wolfdog to tug. Be careful not to raise his head up too high or jerk it around too roughly as you play; let most of the motion come from him.
4. Stop while he still has his teeth on the toy and say "Leave It."
   a. If your wolfdog releases the toy, smile, say, "Thank You" and take the toy. Wait a few seconds, then say, "Take it." Present the toy and resume the game.
   b. If he doesn't release the toy, say "Oh well" in a disappointed tone and take it from him. (With one hand on the toy and the other palm down over his muzzle, squeeze his upper lips near the back teeth gently and remove the toy when his mouth opens.) Put the toy away. The "Leave It" needs more work; address it in a separate training session.
5. When you've decided the game is over, say, "That's all" and put the toy away.

"Who needs those silly humans?"

Note: Tug-of-Woof can also be used to help wolfdogs who are extremely shy and submissive with people, to gain confidence. Try to get your wolfdog to put his mouth on the toy, saying "Take it." When he does, praise him. Gradually work up to shaking it back and forth gently while in his mouth, then let him win. Make a big, happy fuss when he does!

5. **Handling** Handling exercises are a pleasant, non-coercive way to reinforce your leadership status. They are also important, since you should be able to handle your wolfdog physically, for a variety of reasons. You might need to remove a foreign object from his mouth, a pebble from between his toes, or a foxtail (or "sticker") from anywhere on his body. You might want to cut his toenails or to check inside his ears for infection. The point is, you should be able to handle any part of your wolfdog's body, including the ears, mouth and paws. Dominant canines often object to being

8

handled, especially in sensitive areas. However, as you are the one in charge, your wolfdog should come to understand that you have access to his body wherever and whenever you need to.

Whether you are starting out with a pup or an adult, get your wolfdog used to be handled in small, gradual steps. Begin handling exercises when your companion is pleasantly worn out and ready to relax. Sit on the floor with him stretched out on his side if possible. Play some soothing music and burn some calming aromatherapy oil if you'd like. It will relax you both! Massage from his chest down toward his rump using long, open-palmed, gentle strokes. As he begins to show signs of relaxation (i.e. heavy sighs, shift in body position, or general lessening of body tension), stroke the sides of his face, the top of his head, and his back and shoulders, softly at first and then with gentle pressure. Note that we purposely did not begin with the top of the head, shoulders or back, as petting those areas can be considered a dominant act. If he wriggles, simply hold him calmly until he relaxes, and continue.

Once your wolfdog is deeply relaxed, work your way down his legs to the paws. Handle each paw, kneading and gently separating the paw-pads as though you are looking for a pebble in-between. If your wolfdog protests, hold on gently, offering soothing verbal praise when he does allow the touches. Never become angry or forceful. Keep the mood light. To make things easier, if you feel it necessary, keep treats nearby. For each brief touch of a sensitive area, give a treat. (If you are using a clicker—see *Clicker Training* —click as you touch or lightly hold the body part, then treat.)

Other areas which you should be able to handle regularly are the ears and mouth. Holding your wolfdog's ear gently, take a quick peek inside, then praise him. Extend the inspection time as he becomes more comfortable with it. Next, open his mouth by holding one hand palm-down over the top of his muzzle and the other palm-up under his lower jaw, fingers curled. Take a quick peek inside, praising as he allows this, then close. Extend the time his mouth remains open as you practice this exercise over time. Pull your wolfdog's lips up gently to inspect the gums. This is good practice if you plan to brush his teeth. (Yes, many people do brush their canine's canines. There is even doggie toothpaste on the market!) It is also helpful to know what color your wolfdog's gums are normally, as abnormally pale gums are one sign of extreme illness. Another wonderful advantage of handling exercises is that visits to the groomer and veterinarian will be less stressful on your companion and on their staff.

"My, what big teeth you have!"

One last handling exercise, paws-down my personal favorite... A canine who is lying on his back is in a submissive position. This is a good thing, and we want to get him used to being in this posture without feeling threatened. With your wolfdog lying down and relaxed, roll him gently on to his back and give him a tummyrub. If you'd like, sing to him! I have to confess that not only do I sing to my fur-kids while giving tummyrubs, but each has their own special, silly song. Mojo's is sung to the tune of Simon and Garfunkel's *Love me Like A Rock*. It goes like this: "Cause my Mama rubs me/she rubs me/she get down her knees and rub me/well she ru-u-ubs me like a dog/she rubs me like a dog/my Mama she rubs me..." Told ya it was silly! But you know what? Mojo loves it and so do I. And I dare you to try it without breaking into a huge grin. Singing keeps the situation light, and fearful dogs seem to find being in this submissive position less threatening when there is high-pitched happy talk or soft singing going on.

Note: Do not confuse placing your wolfdog on his back with the "alpha roll." There is no force or coercion involved in tummyrubs! Handling should be a pleasant exercise for both of you. If your wolfdog absolutely protests being handled, do not put yourself in danger by attempting it. Employ other leadership tactics first, then come back and try handling again, always exercising caution.

6. **Obedience Training** Training is one of the best ways to teach your wolfdog to pay attention and to respect you as leader. Once he has learned the Sit cue (see *Training Down, Sit and Stay*), you have another tool to reinforce leadership. It's simple. Whenever your wolfdog wants something, ask him to sit first. Have him sit for meals, for treats, before putting the leash on for a walk, before throwing the ball—in short, before anything he finds valuable. In

addition, do brief training sessions throughout the day. Aim for twice-daily, five minute sessions. These can be done before meals if you'd like, so that the meal clearly signals the end of the training session. Training before scheduled feedings is also a good way to train yourself to do sessions regularly.

7. The Long Down-Stay Every canine should learn self-control. Teaching a long down-stay not only accomplishes that goal, but is a wonderful way to reinforce leadership. It also affords some much-deserved "down time" when *you* need it. If your wolfdog doesn't already know them, teach Down and Stay (see *Training Down, Sit and Stay*). Practice down-stays when your wolfdog is naturally tired out. At first, practice with him right next to you; it will be easier for him to stay in a down position that way. Sit on the floor next to him if you'd like. Ask him to lie down, then to stay. If he breaks the stay, you have asked for too much too soon. Get him back into position and start over. If he absolutely can not or will not stay down on his own, even for a few seconds, let him nibble on a treat from your hand, but don't let him grab it. As long as he lays there nibbling, praise and pet him for staying down. If that's not sufficient, place a hand gently over his lower back to keep him in position. Lastly, if all else fails, attach a leash to his collar and keep it under your foot, leaving just enough slack so he can comfortably lie down, but not enough so he can stand up. With each success, extend the down time by a few seconds. Once you've got a solid minute-long down-stay, increase the distance between you by taking one step back. Keep in mind that when you increase distance, you must go back to a shorter stay at first. Build the down-stay gradually over time from three seconds to thirty minutes. (No, that's not a typo—I did say minutes, not seconds, and it can be done!)

If your wolfdog has a bed, have him practice down-stays there while you relax in front of the television or lose yourself in a good book. (Some people, by the way, call the verbal cue for long down-stays "Settle." Use whichever you prefer.) You can also ask for a down-stay while you eat dinner, when you have friends over, or just want a little fur-free time to yourself.

8. **Control Access** Many dominant-type dogs attempt to control access to locations. They do this by lying across doorways and generally blocking your path. Though seemingly innocuous, this behavior is not acceptable. As the leader, you control the resources, and access to space is one of them. If your wolfdog lies across a doorway or is otherwise blocking your way, ask him nicely to move. If he knows "Go to your bed," you might ask him to do so. You could also stand a foot or two away and call him to you. Either of these will effectively get him out of your path. If he complies, praise him and go on your merry way. Problem solved, no confrontation. If he absolutely won't move, say "Oh well" in your best disappointed voice, go directly to the fridge and take out the yummiest food you can find. Show it to him, saying "You could have had this!" Then put it away. I'll bet the next time you ask, he'll move. In fact, I'd make a point of asking him again as soon as possible.

When a higher-ranking wolf passes a lower-ranking pack member who is blocking his path, he gives a gentle bump with his hip; the lower-ranking wolf moves aside. Personal space is a big deal to canines! (It is to people, too. Don't you hate it when someone stands too close behind you in line at the market?) If your wolfdog crosses in front of you as you walk, or is otherwise being a "space invader," use your lower body to *gently* push him aside.

If your wolfdog is especially pushy, make a point of going through doorways first. Practice this by putting him on a sit-stay, opening the door, going through, then calling him out to you. If he gets up as the door opens, calmly close it and begin again. (This is also good practice to prevent door-darting.) You can also use your own body to block and get him to move back from the door. For extremely dominant wolfdogs, be sure you walk ahead even down hallways in your home. Use every opportunity to have him follow you, the pack leader. You could even tether him to you with a leash for a week or two, so he is forced to follow wherever you go.

9. **Neutering** There is no reason, unless you are planning to breed, not to neuter your wolfdog. (And unless you have been breeding for many years, have genetically and temperamentally desirable lines, have a waiting list for pups and will take back any animal your buyers can't keep, you shouldn't even be thinking about it.) Besides, neutering won't cause harm, and could potentially help your leadership status. Wolfdogs who are extremely dominant, aggressive or fearful should absolutely be neutered. Those are traits that should not be passed on. Neutering lowers testosterone levels, and may therefore lower aggression. Neutering will also stop your male wolfdog from wanting to romance every female in the neighborhood who's in heat, and will prevent certain types of cancer.

10. **You Decide** Who makes the decisions in your house? Sometimes it's not so clear-cut. If your wolfdog sits, puts a paw on your knee and gives you those big puppy-dog eyes, and you then pet him, *he's* made the decision that it's time for some affection. *You* should be deciding what happens when, and whether it happens at all. (I know, those big puppy-dog eyes are awfully hard to resist, but try.) You decide, for example, when

14

it's time for a meal. This means that when your wolfdog starts getting antsy and pawing at you around his usual mealtime, you don't respond by getting up and fixing his meal; you do it when you're good and ready. *You* decide when it's time for play; for taking a walk; for a tummyrub; or for lying calmly without doing a thing.

Following this program will go a long way toward establishing leadership. Remember, a wolfdog who knows who's leader and understands his place in the pack is a happy, secure woofer— which makes life together much more pleasant for both of you.

BARF

One of the most common questions that comes up regarding wolfdogs is, "Do they need meat in their diet?" The answer is no, they don't *need* it, insofar as they are able to subsist on a diet of dry kibble alone. If the kibble is high quality, with ingredients the body can use rather than filler which is passed through, many do just fine. Do wolfdogs do *better* with meat in their diet? Ah, now that's another question. Many people, myself included, feel that the answer is yes. In recent years, more and more wolfdog owners have discovered BARF (Bones And Raw Food, or Biologically Appropriate Raw Food). The staple of this natural diet, popularized by Dr. Ian Billinghurst in his book *Give Your Dog A Bone* (see *Resources*), is vitamin-rich, nutritious, raw meat.

Before we discuss the BARF diet, a word about dry kibble. There is a great variation in quality from one brand of kibble to another. Nutritional value is best researched by reading labels. The usual suspects as far as ingredients which are not well tolerated by wolfdogs are corn and soy. Some foods actually list corn as the first ingredient (meaning that is what there is most of). The first two ingredients should ideally be a meat such as chicken or turkey, without the word "meal" or worse, "by-product" after it. "Meat" is the clean flesh of cattle and other animals. "Meat meal" is rendered meal made from animal tissue. "Meat by-product" does not include meat at all, but may include organs, bone and blood. Poultry by-product meal may also include feet and heads.

Check the label to find out what the food is preserved with. It should list vitamins C or E, rather than potentially dangerous preservatives such as BHA, BHT or ethoxyquin (both of which are still commonly used). Bottom line, as each canine is an individual, assess how well your wolfdog is doing on his current diet. Signs of good nutrition include a shiny coat, clear eyes, firm stools and a healthy energy level.

Will Raw Meat Cause My Wolfdog to Eat Grandmothers?

There is a persistent myth that feeding raw meat turns canines into bloodthirsty, aggressive beasts. While a problem might develop if you feed live animals, feeding no-longer-moving raw meat is not a problem. I don't know of a single case where feeding raw meat resulted in any type of behavior problem (besides squabbles over the food in packs who were not yet accustomed to receiving it), and there is certainly no scientific evidence to the contrary.

Some people hesitate to feed raw meat because they fear that their wolfdog will become infected with salmonella. You needn't worry. Canines have a shorter digestive tract than humans, and there is less chance that they will become infected. In the wild, wolves do not contract salmonella from eating raw kill! Although the BARF diet advocates raw meat, if you are truly concerned about parasites (especially if you do not have access to organic foods), boil the meat. Some of the nutrients will be lost, but you will feel safer and the benefits are still many. Or, rinse the meat well with hot water and human grade 30% hydrogen peroxide before serving raw. (The peroxide can be used full strength or diluted, but be sure to rinse well with water afterwards.)

Always be sure to wash your hands very carefully after handling raw meat. Use a disinfectant on any surfaces your hands or the meat might have come in contact with.

Elk-Burger, Hold the Fries!

The BARF diet reflects what wolves eat in the wild. Wolves are, for the most part, carnivores. They eat other animals, thereby consuming meat, organs, bones and even fur. They also eat the contents of their prey's stomach and intestines, which contain plant materials. Your wolfdog is technically an omnivore, meaning he *can* eat meat, vegetables and fruit. According to Dr. Billinghurst, the diet should be varied, as feeding just one type of food item may result in an imbalance. On one-item-only diets, such as organ meats, the wolfdog's appearance may improve for a few months, but the imbalance it creates might show up later as skin problems, arthritis or worse; an organ-meats-only diet has an excess of protein, phosphorus, calories and vitamin A, and is deficient in calcium. Billinghurst warns that feeding a meat-only diet, even in the fairly safe form of cooked meat without the bones (cooked chicken bones can splinter and be fatal), can cause problems such as arthritis, eczema, kidney disease, heart disease and cancer.

What Dr. Billinghurst does recommend is balance and variety. Following the BARF plan, the bulk of your wolfdog's diet would be raw, meaty bones. He suggests that raw chicken backs and/or wings top the list, and mentions lamb, beef and pork as other potential meat sources. *Note: While chicken and turkey can carry salmonella, beef and pork may harbor E. coli bacteria. Beef and pork are also more likely to contain Trichinosis and Cystocerca, which are encysted tapeworms—for these reasons among others, many people prefer to feed chicken and turkey rather than beef or pork.* Another good meat source is marrow bones, often sold in the market as "bones for soup." Raw marrow contains ingredients which help to maintain a healthy immune system. Bones also provide a good outlet for your wolfdog's energy (a good sized raw marrow bone buys at least a half hour of peace and quiet in my house) and are great for keeping teeth free of plaque. Try to obtain your meat through as "clean" a source as possible, such as an organic foods market. There has been concern in recent years about the steroids fed to supermarket-bought chicken, which can be unhealthy to young pups in the long run.

"Eat Your Veggies!"

Here's your chance to get even for all those years you were forced to sit at the table until all your veggies were eaten. You'll like this... you get to pulverize the little suckers! Plant cells are surrounded by a cellulose wall. According to Dr. Billinghurst, a canine's digestive system can not break down the cell wall, so if you don't do it for them by putting raw veggies through a food processor or juicer, most of the nutritional value is not being accessed. Any veggie in season is fair game. Broccoli, spinach, cauliflower, carrots, celery and potatoes are all usable. If you can't find any other way to feed this veggie mixture, try freezing it in small plastic containers and feeding the resulting "vegsicle."

Fruits & More

The main thing to know about fruit is that it should be over-ripe. By serving fruit raw and over-ripe, digestive upsets are avoided. Tropical fruits are particularly nutritious, as they contain high levels of enzymes and anti-oxidants. Other supplements to your wolfdog's diet may include plain yogurt and raw eggs (with the shell, which provides calcium) in small amounts, organ meats (liver, kidneys, heart) and even seafood such as fatty fish, herring and sardines. (As there have been cases of poisoning from raw salmon, I would avoid that particular fish.) Raw meaty bones should make up approximately 50-75% of the diet. Organ meats can account for 5-15%, which roughly translates to feeding organ meats once a week. The rest may consist of raw veggies, fruits, grains and the occasional yogurt and eggs.

There is no way for me to present Dr. Billinghurst's entire plan in one short chapter. If the BARF diet interests you, please research it further. On the internet, typing in BARF at any search engine will yield links to a variety of raw foods-related information. There is also a book by Kymythy Schultze called *Natural Nutrition for Dogs and Cats (*see *Resources)*, which presents a slightly different take on feeding a raw diet. Schultze's approach isn't as tightly structured as Billinghurst's, and some find it easier to follow. Schultze counsels readers not to focus on exact percentages and amounts, but rather on "food groups" and balance.

Many people start with the basics of a raw diet plan, then modify as their lifestyle allows. It takes a little more time and effort to feed raw foods, but the monetary output is comparable to feeding a high-end kibble, and the health benefits to your wolfdogs are priceless.

One Woman's BARF...

Gudrun Dunn has worked with wolfdogs for many years. The remainder of this chapter is Gudrun's own version of a raw foods diet, complete with how-tos and recipes to get you started.

The long-term health of our four-legged friends has always been a top priority for my husband Mike and I. There are a number of factors involved in why some animals live longer than others, but of all those variables, the one we can have the most say in is dietary matters. We feel that the key to enabling an animal to reach the full potential of his genetic inheritance is to not hamper that growth and development through poor nutrition. Therefore with consideration for quality, time and cost we feed our wolfdogs what we believe to be the most appropriate diet for their needs.

The feeding program we've developed for our animals is by far healthier than anything we've found in a bag or can. It's easy to prepare and costs less for us in the long run than a diet based on premium kibble. I judge the results over time by the individual's weight, coat/skin, energy level, fecal properties, veterinary checkups and long-term overall mental and physical well-being.

Generally it can be said that the higher the content range and the more recent the wolf inheritance, the less likely the wolfdog is able to remain solid (not have diarrhea) on kibble alone. But even if my dog's stools are well-formed on kibble, I've found that with all the grain and filler ingredients, unpronounceable additives and heat processing, the animal can tend toward having diet-linked health issues in the long run. It's my opinion that just like dogs, most wolfdogs can survive on a premium kibble based diet high in animal protein. But, I question why *just survive* when the animal can really *thrive* long-term on a more natural raw foods diet?

22

How we feed our wolfdogs is really simple; everything is raw and is based on raw meaty bones. There's no cooking involved! We don't strive to make each meal complete, and we don't follow any set rules other than paying attention to the vitamin and nutritional value of each ingredient, and stool solidifying or loosening properties. I try to balance out what I feed over a period of a week to two weeks, not overloading with too many nutrient sources that won't all get processed at that feeding.

In feeding a variety of content ranges, I've found that everything is dependent on the individual animal's unique dietary needs and preferences. I like to take things on a case-by-case basis and I hope you will too in formulating a good feeding program for your wolfdogs.

We try to find quality organic sources for the raw foods we buy, but if unavailable we grow or raise our own ingredients, or shop around for the best deals on commercial product in bulk. (I figure almost anything raw is better than vitamin-depleted cooked food.) Most of what I buy is human grade (which means it has passed the USDA inspection process) but is cheap, as it may not be anything a human would want to eat. (Raw chicken backs for dinner? Yuck!)

If you have frequent access to fresh roadkill or game, whole carcasses could also be incorporated into a raw foods diet. But do be aware of your local laws, and cautious about poisons, parasites and other nasties. To minimize risk, I avoid feeding wild foods and leave that to whatever small critters the wolfdogs catch inside their enclosures.

Wolfdogs A-Z

Sample Ingredients

Before getting into the nitty-gritty of how I feed, here's a sample listing of what I feed (not all at once!), the typical ingredients of our raw foods feeding program (by design or happenstance):

Apple cider vinegar
Buttermilk
Cottage cheese
Eggs, whole, with or without shell
Flax seed oil, cold pressed
Yogurt, plain with active live cultures or goat's milk
_____

Apples
Bananas, overripe
Blackberries
Blueberries
Grapefruit
Lemons, rind and all
Oranges
Red seedless grapes
Strawberries
Watermelon (for fun)
_____

Asparagus
Baby carrots
Broccoli
Celery
Cilantro
Collard greens
Dandelion greens
Garlic
Green beans, canned, no-salt

Kale
Mustard greens
Parsley
Pumpkin, canned
Spinach
Zucchini

―――――

Beef leg bones (occasional recreational chewing,
not part of diet)
Birds other than domestic meat birds
Canned whole sardines or mackerel
Chicken backs or frames
Chicken necks
Chicken wings
Deer carcass or parts including the hide
Gizzards, chicken or turkey
Hearts
Kidney
Liver, beef mostly
Lizards
Ox tails
Pork neck bones (deep frozen upwards of 10 days)
Rabbit (human-grade only, not wild-caught--parasite
concerns)
Squirrels
Stillborn calves
Turkey necks
Whole fresh fish (except Pacific Salmon--fluke risk)

*No-no's: Onions, chocolate, plants of the nightshade family (i.e.
potato greens), anything to excess.*

The Feeding Program

Don't let that long list overwhelm you! I'd say that about sixty to seventy percent of what we feed is non-weight bearing, raw meaty bones, i.e. mainly chicken frames/backs/necks and turkey necks. Sometimes with the fat stripped off, sometimes not. Super simple.

I do use some ground beef or turkey as a means of adding vegetables and other supplements to the diet. Comparatively, there's very little plain muscle meat in what I feed my animals. I find that muscle meat alone is "cheating;" there's very little of the essential nutrients and vitamins that are found in raw bone and cartilage. By "other supplements" I mean cold-pressed flax seed oil, raw egg, apple cider vinegar, fruits for vitamin C and other lesser ingredients that are important but don't make up the bulk of the diet.

As mentioned, what we feed most of is chicken frames or backs. These include a tiny bit of organ meat and a good ratio of edible bone/cartilage to muscle meat and skin/fat. But if I feed chicken backs and baby carrots for a week straight, the following week I'll feed organ meats and vegetables one meal with turkey necks the following feeding (we feed twice a day), and repeat this for a few days before feeding all turkey necks for a few days. Too much organ meat or green leafy vegetables in one feeding can bring on loose stools, so I like to firm them up with the necks. That is the key to figuring out the combination of what to feed in daily meals: knowing which food items are stool-loosening (i.e. beef kidney) and which are stool-firming (i.e. whole baby carrots, or grated).

Turkey necks, which don't usually come with skin attached, are quite lean. I've found I must compensate a mostly turkey neck diet with other fat/oil sources and more organ meats than a mostly chicken frames diet.

The organ meats I use most often are beef liver, kidney and heart, and chicken gizzards, liver and heart. Heart and gizzards are multi-purpose and hard to classify, but beef heart in particular (which is more a high quality muscle meat than an organ meat) is very nutritious and somewhat fattier than other organ meats. That helps to know when combining beef heart with other foods.

Another important consideration in how we feed is *moderation*; too much of anything is never good. For example, raw fresh spinach is a good source of iron and vitamin A, but too much in the diet interferes with the body's ability to absorb calcium. Small amounts every so often are quite beneficial, but wouldn't be if fed everyday.

I strongly caution against feeding weight-bearing bones (i.e. legs, thighs) as these tend to be harder, are more likely to crack off in chunks that can lodge internally causing harm, and may chip or crack your canine's teeth. Very rarely do we give our animals large beef marrow bones. These bones are not part of the diet; they're only for occasional recreational chewing.

With the exception of pumpkin, maybe some green beans, sardines and mackerel, I do not tend to feed canned foods. The canning process involves steaming or cooking, which defeats the purpose of feeding a raw diet. Pure canned pumpkin is good for stuffing in Kong toys (see *Kongs and Other Sanity Preservers - NW*) and helping to firm stools. Canned whole sardines or mackerel in water are valuable for the fish oils, but be aware of the salt content.

Busy or Lazy?

Most of what I feed is refrigerator temperature, or is warmed slightly to take the chill off. Some canines don't care, while others seem to be just as picky about the temperature of their meals as some felines can be.

On days when I've forgotten to take food out of the freezer the night before, I either rapid defrost (setting a bag full of turkey necks in the garage in the morning to thaw for evening feeding, or running it under warm water), or feed the meal frozen if all else fails.

I don't use the microwave to defrost raw meaty bones, as it doesn't take much heat to change the way those bones crack. Poultry bones in particular seem to "cook" before the meat itself thaws, so I just avoid the microwave altogether. Not worth the risk of splintering bones, in my opinion.

Sometimes I feed canned Innova dog food with baby carrots, an egg, raw chicken meat, flax seed oil, fruit bits or other raw ingredients and supplements tossed in. This works in a pinch and does not seem to upset my canines' tummies as much as dried kibble does.

Other times I prepare some rather interesting concoctions. On the following page you'll find two of my favorites!

"Green Fishy"

Ingredients:
Two 15 oz. cans water-packed mackerel (drained)
1 can water-packed tuna (also drained)
Large handful washed raw spinach leaves
Some parsley
A few baby carrots
1/2 clove garlic

Whirl in the Cuisinart or blender while adding water. Thicken with baby rice.

(I'll feed this at the first feeding, and will feed something more stool-firming later in the evening.)

"Kitchen Sink Frozen Block Treat or Meal"

Ingredients: Anything that can be frozen (leftover Green Fishy or strawberries, bananas, chunks of venison... creativity is key.)

Take one large plastic tub, put about an inch of water in it, freeze. Place food item (preferably pre-frozen) on the ice with a portion of it resting on the side of the container. (By placing the food item against the side of the tub, once the block is out of the tub the food is exposed to air and can be sniffed, scratched, gnawed and licked out.) Pour another layer over, being careful not to float the frozen food item. Once solid, pour more water over it to form block. To remove block from container, pour warmed water over it. *(This is great for hot weather as a treat, or, make the food item plentiful enough to constitute a full meal.)*

If I'm truly out of ideas and have no raw meaty bones defrosted, for our fully-mature wolfdogs only, I'll just fast them that day. I've never known there to be any harm in fasting a healthy, mature wolfdog for a day or three. As long as they have access to clean water at all times and are in good health, withholding food for a short while is a nice way to cleanse the internal workings. I start them back on food with a dollop of active-culture yogurt, and don't overfeed them that first day back on solids.

Tips for Newcomers to Raw Feeding

If you're just starting to feed raw meaty bones to your young critters, I suggest you stick with raw chicken necks in the beginning. Or if the animal is larger, chicken backs or turkey necks. Chicken tends to be easiest for most animals to process, and most importantly, in time, chewing these softer bones will develop both jaw muscles and good chewing habits as well as give digestive enzymes a chance to kick in. If raw chicken or turkey necks are not available go for chicken wings, but be sure to pop the joint before feeding it. (First-time chewers may swallow wings whole. If you dislocate the joint it may be safer, not forming an A-shape in the throat.)

Vegetables and fruits tend to loosen stools and should be fed in moderation. When you're in the beginning stages of raw feeding, go easy on your animal's digestive system. Variety is necessary, but go slowly to get a feel for what types and amounts of veggies and fruits your animal can handle. Grated or whole sweet baby carrots seem palatable to most canines, as does a small amount of canned pumpkin. Over time, you could gradually add small amounts of torn raw leafy greens such as dandelion, parsley, and so on. Fruit should be given very sparingly at first, maybe half a handful of blueberries or half of an overripe banana.

Risk Factors

The most common question I am asked in regard to feeding a raw meaty bones-based diet is, "Aren't you afraid of giving your animals internal parasites?" The answer is yes, that is a concern of mine, which is why I make an effort to purchase good quality human-grade meaty bones, and why I make sure to freeze certain items and take other safe handling measures. I also make it a habit to wash everything before feeding it to remove wax and preservatives, fecal matter, viruses and bacteria.

I also weigh the consequences of not feeding raw foods to my animals. Without the addition of real foods to their diet, I'd be sentencing some of my dogs and wolfdogs to a life of chronic diarrhea, inadequate protein/nutrient levels, and the long-term health effects thereof. The health risks involved with not feeding an appropriate diet are far too risky for me.

In all the years I have fed raw, not a single one of my animals has developed problems related to the diet; no GI tract obstructions, no gastric torsion, no internal parasite infestations... just good health.

I hope you enjoy the same success.

Clicker Training

Though clicker training has been around for a long time, it's only recently gained real popularity for training pet canines. Karen Pryor, one of the first champions of clicker training, employed its principles when working with dolphins. Many trainers of exotic and marine mammals use it. And recently, more books and videos have become available which teach clicker training for pet canines. (See *Resources* for some excellent ones.)

Remember those small tin crickets that sold for 29 cents at the local party shop? Those are clickers. Of course, today's clickers are better made and a bit more expensive. Rather than pushing your wolfdog into position and then saying, "Good boy" (the traditional "modeling" approach), clicker training teaches him to think for himself and actually *offer* behaviors. (*Hmm,* you're probably wondering, *do I really want Timber to think for himself more than he already does?* I hear you.) Actually, clicker training is excellent for wolfdogs in particular, as most wolfdogs are extremely intelligent and catch on quickly. It also provides mental stimulation, which is not only healthy, but more tiring than you might think. And of course, a pleasantly tired-out woofer gets into way less trouble than a wound-up one!

The Trick's in the Click

The idea behind clicker training is that *the click marks the exact moment the desired behavior is taking place.* That's why the click is called a "marker." If you were teaching your wolfdog to sit, for example, you would click at the exact second his rear touched the ground. You may be wondering what the advantage is of clicking, versus just praising, "Good boy!" For one thing, a click is much more precise. Let's say you wanted to teach your wolfdog

33

to tilt his head on cue (a very cute trick, by the way); the instant his head was tilted, you would click. What are the chances that you could catch that split-second of head-tilt with verbal praise? Very slim. It has actually been proven that the motor reflex to move our thumb to click is faster than our verbalization response time. Take it from a fast-talking ex-New Yorker, it's true. Plus, our verbal tone varies due to a variety of factors (i.e. stress, excitement), while the click always sounds the same.

Of course, a click is not something any canine is born wanting to work for. It needs to be paired with a reward—you guessed it, a food treat. For each click, the wolfdog earns a treat, i.e. a piece of hot dog. Most catch on to this concept very quickly. It makes you wonder if there isn't some scientific correlation between the presence of hot dogs and a fast upward learning curve. Perhaps hot dogs should carry the label, "Warning: The contents of this package may greatly influence your canines' ability to learn!"

Getting Started

Let's get your wolfdog associating the click with the treat, and give you some practice at coordinating clicking and treating. As wolfdogs can be sensitive to sharp sounds, take care when you first introduce yours to the clicker. Most clickers are fairly loud. Take wolfdog, clicker and treats outdoors or to an indoor area that does not have loud acoustics. Make sure there are no distractions. Put the clicker in your pocket, and muffle the sound further by wrapping your hand around it. Clicker in hand, treats in the other, click, count one second, then treat. Repeat. Be sure to click and treat when your wolfdog is in a variety of positions, so he doesn't inadvertently think he's being clicked for a certain behavior, i.e. sitting. You'd be surprised at how quickly canines make associations. You'll know your wolfdog has associated the click with the treat when, after you click, he looks toward the hand with the treats in it. Once your wolfdog is comfortable with the sound of the clicker, take it out of your pocket. You don't need to muffle it. Oh, and don't point the clicker at your wolfdog. Though it may seem like it at times, it's not a remote control!

> For wolfdogs who are very sound-sensitive, i.e. for whom even a muffled click is too startling, use an alternative clicker, such as a ball-point pen. If your wolfdog freaks out over *any* object you try to use, you may substitute the verbal marker, "Yes!" for the click. Just be sure to say "Yes!" in a short, excited burst.

Touch the Stick, Earn a Click: Targeting

Targeting is a fun way to get your wolfdog tuned in to clicker training and for you to see immediate results. You'll need a "target stick" for this exercise. A target stick can be any long, thin dowel-shaped rod, approximately two feet long. A piece of bamboo works well. Look around and see what you have that fits the description, making sure it's not something that will scare your wolfdog. (Target sticks are also available by mail order; or, purchase a thin dowel at your local building supplies store.)

If you can manage it, hold both the target stick and clicker in one hand, treats in the other. If not, hold the clicker in one hand, stick in the other, and keep treats handy in a bait bag, pocket or on a nearby table. (I know, a third hand would be helpful here.) Position the target stick so that one end is close to and slightly under your wolfdog's nose. More than likely, he will sniff it. At the moment his nose touches the stick, click! Then treat. Though treats should be delivered a second or so after the click, remember that *the timing of the click is more important than the timing of the treat.* The click gives your wolfdog the information he needs. The treat is simply a reward. If you absolutely can't get to the treat quickly, use a phrase such as "Good boy, we're gonna get a treat for that, yes, good boy!" while you get the treat out. This is called a *verbal bridge*, as your words bridge the gap between behavior and reward, so they are associated with each other. Repeat the exercise. If your wolfdog does not sniff the stick, try moving it around or urging "What's that?" to make it more interesting. I have seen very few canines *not* want to sniff the target stick. If yours happens to be one of them, try rubbing something yummy on the end of the stick like hot dogs to make it more interesting. (Yes, hot dogs are my answer to most things in life!)

Of course, knowing our little darlings as we do, we also want to be especially careful to click just as nose touches stick and not after—we don't want the sniff to turn into an open-mouthed inspection, leading to the untimely demise of the poor stick. *(Tip: For wolfdogs who keep biting the stick, place a styrofoam ball, too large for your wolfdog to mouth, on the end of it.)* Once your wolfdog is interested in the touch game, move the target stick into different positions, clicking and treating each time he touches it. Hold it out to the side where he can reach it, and down near the ground. Be careful about holding it directly above his head, as many wolfdogs are fearful of overhead objects. *Note: If your wolfdog touches the stick in the middle rather than at the tip, that's fine. Eventually, begin to click only for those touches that are closer to the end. Work toward clicking only for tip touches.* Once your wolfdog is successfully performing this exercise each time the stick is offered, add the cue, "Touch" *as he moves to touch it.* He will quickly come to associate the word with the action. After many successful repetitions in this manner, present the stick and say "Touch" *before* he moves to touch the stick.

A cue is the same as what has traditionally been called a *command*. It just sounds less... well, *military*. I prefer to ask my canines for behaviors, rather than demanding them.

Once your wolfdog is really into targeting the stick, try this: With your wolfdog by your side, walk forward holding the stick at waist level, target end extending out toward him. Be sure he can reach it comfortably without jumping up or crowding you. Click and treat each time he touches it. Wow! Who'da thought? Your fur-kid is doing a perfect heel! Try to click and treat *as* you walk together, so it's clear that walking alongside you in that position is what earns the click. Once your wolfdog is following and touching the stick, over time, begin to fade the use of the stick. Shorten the length so that the tip is closer to your body (just pull it closer in), to the point where it eventually disappears altogether. You could add a verbal cue such as "Follow" when you start the exercise.

One of the wonderful things about clicker training is that it puts the animal in charge. After all, their behavior causes the human to click and give them a treat! Pretty neat stuff for animals, compared to being yanked around or pushed into position, don'tcha think? Most tend to get very excited once they learn the rules of the game, and thoroughly enjoy playing. It's wonderful to see that "light bulb" go on in a canine's mind when they really "get" clicker training and begin to offer behaviors.

Targeting can be used as a foundation to teach many different behaviors, and is even helpful for changing behavior problems. For example, targeting can be used to help fearful wolfdogs. Teach a fearful wolfdog to target the back of your hand instead of the stick. Then invite a friend over. Play the targeting game with your hand, then with theirs. Your wolfdog will learn that people are fun, not scary. If your wolfdog is too frightened to try this, go slow and practice desensitizing him to people separately from training sessions. (See *Fear Issues*.)

Targeting can be used as a distraction in situations where your wolfdog is becoming tense, i.e., passing a barking dog behind a fence, or waiting at the vet's office. It is also useful for teaching a variety of tricks. (See *Take a Bow Wow* videos in *Resources*.) In our little pack, Mojo, though much loved, was never thought to be extremely bright—especially by my husband. So, I began clicker training him (Mojo, not the husband). He caught on very quickly. I began to secretly teach Mojo tricks, just to watch my husband's reaction when Mojo and I showed them off. One evening hubby and I we were sitting on the couch watching television. I casually looked over at Mojo and said, "Mojo, turn off the lights." The look on my husband's face when Mojo ran to the light switch and turned it off with his nose was priceless. Mojo loves clicker training and so does Mom!

The more you practice clicker training, the better you and your wolfdog will get at it. Don't worry if your coordination or timing isn't great at first. Unlike punishment-based training, you won't hurt anything if your timing is off and you won't "ruin" your wolfdog. As your timing improves, which specific behavior you're asking for will become clearer, and his performance will improve.

You may find that when working on a new behavior, your wolfdog will offer other behaviors he's already been taught. I often work with Soko, my German Shepherd, and Mojo at the same time. (I don't recommend working with two canines at once unless at least one has a really good down-stay.) There is nothing funnier than watching the two of them offer spins, crawls ("Commando" as we call it), and more when they're not sure what Mom wants. They only know they really want to earn that click! If you're reading this and thinking *my wolfdog could never learn that stuff*, remember Mojo. Trust me, if he can do it, your fur-kid can. Mojo has been taught these tricks with the clicker, among others: Spin, Walk Backwards, Commando, Wave, Play Dead, Tilt Your Head

and of course, Turn out the Lights. We're currently working on Say Your Prayers, where he puts both paws up on a chair and lowers his head. It's very cute! Now if I could only teach him to make coffee in the morning...

Wolfdogs A-Z

The Shape of Things to Come

Clicker training is an easy, effective way to shape behavior. *Shaping* means breaking a behavior down into small increments, then rewarding for and building on each small success along the way. To illustrate, let's teach your wolfdog to "Go To Bed." Here's how I would do it:

Sit with your wolfdog in the general vicinity of his bed. Have clicker ready, treats close at hand. The first piece of behavior we are going to click for is your wolfdog simply looking at the bed. If you're sitting close enough to it, he may do this on his own. Just wait. If he doesn't look after a period of time, it's perfectly okay to draw his attention to it by tossing a treat on the bed. As soon as he looks toward the bed, click and treat. Of course, if you've tossed a treat, he's probably gone all the way to the bed to get it. That's okay. Click as he touches the bed. (Once he gets the idea that looking toward or moving toward the bed earns a click, each time you reward, toss the treat *away* from the bed, to set him up for the next repetition.) Continue the exercise, clicking for any interest in or movement toward the bed. After a few repetitions, you should see the light go on in your wolfdog's head ("*Ah,* that's *what makes her click!*") and he will begin to move more purposefully toward the bed. Don't worry if he doesn't "get it" right away. Some canines simply take more time than others.

Following is an example of criteria I would click for in shaping "Go To Bed," meaning go to your bed and lie down. Clicking at each step would be contingent on your wolfdog having done the previous ones successfully. In other words, after each step was performed successfully a few times, you would withhold the click the following time, until your wolfdog did just a little bit more. However, if he skips a few steps in the progression, i.e. goes

40

from looking at to standing on the bed, great! Take it! Click and continue from there. Steps to click for might be:

1. Looking at the bed
2. Any movement toward the bed, even one step
3. Further movement toward the bed
4. Approaching the bed
5. Touching the bed with any part of his body
6. Putting at least one paw on the bed
7. Putting two paws on the bed
8. Standing on the bed
9. Standing on the bed, lowering head
10. Standing on the bed, lowering head and elbows to the bed
11. Lying down on the bed
12. Remaining in a lying down position on the bed

Of course, if your wolfdog already knows the cue for lying down, you could, after he gets to the point where he's standing on the bed, give the cue to lie down. Once he's successfully going to the bed and lying down, you would begin to add the cue "Go To Bed" just as he begins to perform the behavior. Very soon you would be able to say "Go To Bed" first, to elicit the behavior.

Note: The criteria I've given are meant to give a general idea of how to shape a behavior. You may find yourself doing it slightly differently, clicking for smaller or larger increments. That's fine! The bottom line is, *get the behavior*. As long as you're not using punishment, it doesn't really matter exactly *how* you get it. Be creative!

Adding Cues

It seems strange to some to add a verbal cue *after* the behavior has already been learned. It's no wonder, as traditional training has always taught just the opposite. To illustrate the advantage of giving the cue *after* a behavior is learned, let me to share an exercise I do with my first-night dog training students. I choose a victim... er, *volunteer*. They play the dog; I'm the trainer. We stand facing each other. I look at them, and in a pleasant voice, say, "Salava!" The "dog" inevitably looks at me like I'm crazy. "Salava," I insist, a bit more sternly this time. The poor dog doesn't know what to do, and begins to get frustrated. "This is a very stubborn dog," I inform the class, and give the cue once more, now in a demanding, almost angry tone. This dog is obviously choosing not to obey me! What can I do with such a willful woofer? Should I shake it? Alpha roll it? Wait! I take a piece of candy and hold it over the person's head. They reach up for it with both hands. "Good dog!" I encourage, and give them the candy. Finally, some progress! After a few successful repetitions, I say "Salava!" just as the person reaches up for the treat. Very soon I can say "Salava!" and they know exactly what I want, and respond correctly. We have successfully put the reaching up behavior on cue. Besides getting the whole class rolling on the floor laughing, this exercise illustrates the pointlessness of us standing there commanding, "Sit!" or "Get down from the sofa!" when the wolfdog has no clue what the words mean. To them, we might as well be shouting, "Timberwolves have landed on Mars!" *By adding the cue once the behavior is already established, we set the wolfdog up to succeed.* A good rule of thumb is to add the cue after you have gotten 20-50 successful repetitions of the behavior.

A common question is, "Will I have to carry the clicker around with me forever?" Absolutely not. Once your wolfdog understands and reliably performs a behavior whenever you ask, in any situation or location, you don't need to use the clicker for it. You may also begin to substitute a verbal, "Yes!" (or a cluck of the tongue) for the click. In other words, "Yes!" becomes the marker. "Yes!" comes in handy too when you don't have a clicker with you but your wolfdog has done something so adorable you want to "capture" the behavior. *Capturing* a behavior with the clicker is like taking a snapshot of it. Your wolfdog does a cute head-tilt to the side—click! You've captured the behavior without luring it or shaping it. If you capture that behavior a few more times, he may well begin to offer it on his own. Eventually, you can give the behavior a name, or cue.

More and more trainers are now offering classes in clicker training. I encourage you to explore this method, whether in a group class, private lessons, or through the many wonderful books and videos available. (See *Resources* for books, videos, clickers and target sticks.) Have fun, and a big *click* to you for caring enough to train your wolfdog!

Dominance Challenges
(And Other Not-So-Fun Stuff)

You may have noticed that this book takes a positive approach to interacting with wolfdogs, and for that matter, all canines. The ideal scenario in dealing with behavior problems would be to prevent them from ever happening to begin with. Socialization, gentle, positive training methods and management go a long way. But realistically, we must be prepared that despite our best efforts, things like dominance challenges and testing can and do occur, especially with rescue animals or those just coming into sexual maturity. The more we understand about how to deal with challenges, the better our chances of preserving a healthy human-canine relationship.

I recently received an e-mail which said, to paraphrase, "My wolfdog will be a year old next week. I know I should expect a dominance challenge. What should I do when it happens?" This person had gotten the idea that all wolfdogs will absolutely challenge their owners at the age of exactly one year. Luckily, that little bit of (probably misconstrued) information is not true. What is true, especially with higher content wolfdogs, is that you may well see incidences of testing behavior as they mature. Low to mid content wolfdogs (and even doggie-dogs) may or may not display this behavior, but it is wise to be prepared. I know a woman who has raised and rescued wolfdogs for years, who swears her low-to-mid content wolfdog challenged her more severely and often than any of the high contents she'd ever lived with.

The best defense is a good offense. Whether you are raising your wolfdog from a pup or taking in a rescue animal, set up clear leadership guidelines from the start. If you haven't already done

45

so, turn to the *Alpha* chapter and read over the suggested leadership strategies. The more certain your wolfdog is that you are fulfilling the role of leader, the more secure he will feel in his own position. *Note: Always use caution when introducing leadership strategies with an adult or rescued animal; introduce new "rules" slowly and gently. Changing everything at once can cause stress, which can result in even worse behavior problems.* Keep in mind too that spaying or neutering your wolfdog at an early age may also help to curb over-the-top "dominant" behavior.

Pups are not as likely to challenge their owners as are adults. Think about a young human child. They accept the fact that Mom and Dad make the rules, and for the most part, they follow along. Now, fast forward to the teenage years. (I can see you parents out there cringing!) Teenagers begin to question the "pack order" and just about everything else around them. Think of young wolfdogs as teenagers with bigger teeth. They probably won't flat-out challenge you, but they may well begin testing you. The teenage-to-young adult years in a wolfdog are roughly between nine and eighteen months of age.

Testing, One, Two...

There is a definite distinction between testing and challenging. Testing is less severe. A test can be anything from a wolfdog crowding your personal space or bumping you while walking by (as higher-ranking wolves do to lower-rankers), to darting in and nipping you from behind, then running off. Tests are subtle (though that nip might not feel so subtle at the time), and are designed to gauge your reaction. It is important to recognize a test for what it is and to respond properly so that the behavior does not escalate.

Please use caution and common sense when using any of the methods which follow:

When hip-bumped, you could stand your ground, or gently shove right back. Crowding your personal space can be easily resolved as well. If you're sitting on something higher than the wolfdog, fold your arms, hunch your shoulders and lean forward; turn slightly to one side, then *gently* push the woof off with your shoulder/upper arm. You are effectively reclaiming your personal space. (If your wolfdog is "testy," don't sit on the ground with him until these issues are resolved.) A nip from behind is a bit more serious. My personal method of dealing with it is, if the woofer is close enough, to whip around, place my hand palm-down across his muzzle and say in a low, stern voice, "No teeth on Mom!" Know your own wolfdog. If you can get away with a stern verbal reprimand only, use it. *I do not recommend scruff-shaking or alpha-rolling your wolfdog.* Remember, aggression begets aggression, and by using those methods, you may escalate what was a simple test into something much more serious, risking injury to yourself and the erosion of your relationship.

Much is made of wolfdogs who have an "alpha" or dominant temperament. Keep in mind that dominance relates to a specific relationship with another animal or person. In other words, your wolfdog may be dominant over other canines in his pack, but submissive toward you and other people.

While testing is indirect, dominance challenges are more serious and are most definitely direct. A dominance challenge is a bid for control. While a test might involve an opportunistic nip from behind, a challenge could entail a wolfdog rearing up on hind legs facing you, placing paws on your shoulders, and growling in your face. Hackles may be raised, lips may be pulled back in a snarl, and the tail may be held high, wagging stiffly. You might find yourself eye-to-eye with a hard, direct stare. Though dominance challenges seemingly come out of nowhere, there is always a reason. Sometimes the owner just hasn't noticed the subtle testing that has been taking place, or has downplayed the importance of it. Sometimes wolfdogs challenge their owners when hormonal changes occur during the winter months (see *Winter Wolf Syndrome*). Even neutered wolfdogs may display this behavior.

Some high content wolfdogs and pure wolves, neutered or not, display changes in temperament as they age. They may begin to challenge people they previously accepted. Or, they still accept those people they know from puppyhood, but new people are fair game. I know of two cases personally where the three-to-four year old adult wolves in question will not let unfamiliar people into their enclosure without challenging them. They are fine with folks they already know, but that's it. Fortunately, their caretakers realize this and don't let new people in with them.

What To Do

So, on to the million dollar question: What should you do if your wolfdog flat-out challenges you? First, don't panic. Breathe. I know, it's easy to say and much harder to do—but staying calm really is the key. *Do not under any circumstances react in kind*, i.e. try to physically dominate a wolfdog who is already in a state of heightened adrenaline-rush arousal. You'll lose. The goal is to get out of the situation safely with dignity intact so that your wolfdog does not feel he's "won." How exactly do you do that? There are so many variables involved that it would be impossible to recommend one simple solution that would work in every circumstance. Nevertheless, here are some suggestions that may help: If you are in an enclosure, act disgusted. As calmly and slowly as possible, still facing your wolfdog but not staring directly at him (that would be a challenge), get out. You might try using calming signals to diffuse the situation, such as a yawn (just don't show your teeth while yawning), turning your head and body slightly away, averting your gaze, or licking your lips. (More on calming signals in *Understanding Body Language and Signals*.) Another option would be to distract the wolfdog from what he is doing. If possible, offer something he can hold in his mouth—after all, your skin and the object can't both be in his mouth—or toss something he can run after, giving you the time to safely leave. If he has teeth on your arm or any other body part, be very careful about pulling back. Skin tears easily. See if you can get him to release by offering something else he can put in his mouth instead, or by getting him to relax. Diffuse the situation. Try to appear unconcerned and happy, even silly, rather than tense and fearful.

Once a dominance challenge has occurred, will your wolfdog act differently toward you? Not if you've handled it calmly and correctly. The next time you interact with him, try to be as relaxed as possible. Act as though nothing had happened. Gradually and carefully, begin to implement a leadership program.

Of course, there is a major difference between a dominance challenge, in which the wolfdog doesn't really want to hurt you but does want you to know he's considering running for the presidency, and an actual attack. In an aggressive, full-out attack, all bets are off. (By a full-out attack I do not mean that your

49

wolfdog simply bites you and moves away. I mean he actually *attacks* you without backing off.) If you can get out without injury to either one of you, great. If not, do whatever you have to do. Afterwards, reflect as objectively as possible on why the attack may have occurred (i.e. medical problems on either of your parts, a stressor in the environment, a changing relationship with other pack members, a previously unnoticed escalation in testing behavior).

Naturally, an animal who flat-out attacks you is one that you should reconsider sharing your life with. Consider your options carefully. One course of action would be to work with someone who is experienced in wolf behavior, or is at least a very good canine trainer. You would then have a professional opinion as to whether these issues are workable. If you're considering giving the animal up, keep in mind that adopting out to someone else is not an option, as you would only be passing the problem along. It's possible that a rescue center might take him, but most are perpetually full, and understandably don't prefer to take in aggressive animals. Euthanasia is a last resort. The decision should never be made lightly or in a state of panic right after an attack, and should only be considered if all other options have been exhausted or if the animal presents a real danger.

Challenging Circumstances

Monty Sloan, Wolf Behavior Specialist at Wolf Park, sheds light on the phenomenon of testing/challenging behaviors: "Popular accounts would have you believe that a pet wolfdog will take the first opportunity to challenge, even attack its owner. The reality is much more complex than this. Although a wolf is open to challenging a dominant pack member, including a human 'pack member,' this will generally only occur under certain circumstances." Sloan lists these as:

- The animal is maturing sexually and is testing and achieving dominance over other canine pack members;
- The animal is fence-fighting with a non-pack member and, already highly aroused, redirects aggression on a person in the pen;
- The animal has a history of aggression and has learned to challenge people;
- The animal becomes overly stimulated during an excited greeting and "boils over" to an aggressive state;
- The animal is kept in an inadequately small pen, leading to boredom and excitability and/or is not worked with, socialized and trained adequately; (See *Enrichment.*)
- The owner trips/falls, is suddenly/conspicuously vulnerable;
- The owner develops a fear of the animal and acts conspicuously vulnerable or afraid;
- The owner rewards aggression in the animal or allows aggressive behaviors to continue unabated;
- The owner fails to understand and compensate for seasonal aggression. This is especially common for males; and/or
- The owner triggers a critical reaction by trying to force the animal to do something, or puts the animal into a situation where the animal becomes defensive.

Sloan offers, "There are numerous other possible situations, but these seem the most common and most are based on a lack of understanding of the animal's social needs and lack of proper training. In Photo A, two 'wolfdogs' are greeting a teenager. Both animals were sold to the owner as having a similar wolf content, about ¾ wolf. However, the one on the right, their first animal, is most likely a dog. Besides looking like a dog, she was a good house pet, was easy to train and did not test people. The other, younger female, is over half wolf and is testing the teenager. Although it was not the case here, such 'testing' *is* perceived by some owners as 'play,' but *it is not play*; it is quite serious and can lead to a bite or even an attack if not modified through proper training. Although she took a lot of work and training, this animal continues to do well years later; but, due to the heightened social aggression between female wolves, she is no longer living with any other female canines.

Even small pups can be seen to show increased testing over and above that seen in dogs. In Photo B, this 10-week-old pure wolf pup was not being overtly aggressive, which would be very unusual at this age, but he *was* incessantly jumping up on this child, pulling at his hair, his collar and his sleeves in an apparent attempt to pull him over. Although this pup was very submissive to adults, he would not submit to the child, and his testing was intense enough that after a few minutes the child had to be taken out of the pup's reach."

~~~~~~~~~~~~~~~~~~~~~~~~~~~~~~

So there you have it. The purpose of this section is not to frighten you or to portray wolfdogs as vicious, evil beasts who spend their time lying in wait for an opportunity to overthrow your rule; but an ounce of prevention is definitely worth a pound of flesh. It is important that you understand wolf behavior and that your animal, being part wolf, *may* display some of these behaviors. So be prepared. Work with your wolfdog on training, implement a leadership program, and always treat him with kindness and respect.

Photo A

Photo B

Enrichment

The dictionary definition of *enrichment* is "to make better or richer." Why should we be concerned about making our wolfdogs' lives better or richer? Because we love them and want them to be happy, of course! A less obvious reason is that a wolfdog who has an interesting life filled with things to do is less likely to be doing things we *don't* want him to do—like digging dirt-condos or munching garden hoses.

Whether your wolfdog shares your home or lives in an outdoor enclosure, there are ways to enrich his life. Here are some ideas...

Find a Friend

If your wolfdog is an only child, consider getting him a friend. Wolves and dogs are pack animals, with a real need to socialize. A canine companion need not be another wolfdog, but should preferably be a canine of the opposite sex, of similar size and

compatible temperament (i.e. if your fur-kid is a pushy, alpha type, don't get another dominant woofer). Be sure both are spay/neutered. Why not same-sex pairs? Males often get into rank issues with other males. Females with females can be a lethal combination. (Think office politics—and ladies, you know what I mean.) Just because your wolfdog has a friend, however, don't assume they're romping around all day amusing each other. You'll still need to provide...

Exercise

Adequate exercise is one of the most important things you can give your wolfdog. Malamutes and Siberian Huskies are two of the most common breeds found in wolfdog mixes. Both were bred to pull heavy loads, which takes a lot of physical exertion. Huskies are a high-energy breed. Combine those tidbits with the fact that pure wolves can trot at nine miles per hour for hours at a time, run at speeds up to 35-40 mph and live in territories that span over 800 square miles, and you've got a canine with a serious need for exercise!

As a professional dog trainer, I work with people whose canine companions have a variety of problems which could be easily be solved or at least toned down by the dog getting more exercise. Any canine with an overabundance of energy will find some way to expend that energy, often in ways we're not wild about. When asked whether their dog gets daily exercise, owners are quick to reply, "Yes, of course!" But when asked exactly *what* the dog does for exercise, they often answer, "I take him for a walk" or "He runs around the yard all day." Taking a walk is certainly good exercise for us, but is most likely not enough exercise for a healthy wolfdog. They need to run! As far as running around the yard all day, canines who are left alone for hours may well sleep during that time. Alternately, some dig, howl or try to escape. What they *don't* generally do is entertain themselves by romping happily for hours on end, flinging their toys around with wild abandon. Even wolfdogs who have a canine companion are not likely to be playing for extended periods.

If your wolfdog(s) are in the yard all day, set aside some time for play when you come home. If your fur-kid plays retrieve games (and I don't mean the ever-popular, Get-The-Ball-And-Eat-It, I mean actually bringing it back to you), throw the ball for him. Get him moving. If you both know the proper rules for Tug-Of-Woof (see *Alpha*), get a game going. Get that energy out! If your wolfdog is great around other dogs and has a solid recall (he comes to you when called), take him to an enclosed park and let him run. (*Do not let him run loose in an unenclosed area no matter how well behaved you think he is, or how strongly you believe he'd never run away. Accidents happens swiftly and irrevocably.*) Many wolfdog owners bring their companions to lakes to let them swim. Most woofers love it. Some bicycling enthusiasts attach a hands-free device so their wolfdog can run along beside them. (If you try this, be careful and start slow so you don't get pulled

over.) Whatever your daily physical activities, consider whether there's a way to include your wolfdog. Once he begins to get more exercise, you will be happily surprised at how much calmer he is in general, and how quickly a variety of "behavior problems" disappear.

Mental Stimulation

Mental stimulation is just as important and at least as tiring as physical exercise. (What would tire *you* out more: thirty minutes of walking or thirty minutes of calculus?) Training your wolfdog is a wonderful way to get brain cells firing (theirs *and* yours). Lessons need not be long. A few five minute, fast-paced sessions spread throughout the day is plenty. Clicker training in particular (see *Clicker Training*) is a great way to get your wolfdog to engage his mental capacities. You might be surprised to find just *how* tired out your companion is after a session.

Training need not be strictly obedience. Teach your wolfdog a trick or two! It's fun, challenging, and you can show off your brilliant woofer to friends (see *Take a Bow Wow* videos in *Resources*). Trick training can even provide solutions to behavioral problems. For example, a wolfdog who overwhelms people with teeth and paws at the front door can be taught to sit and wave, or to fetch a favorite toy each time the doorbell rings.

For a training exercise that will wear your wolfdog out physically, have a rousing round of "puppy pushups." (Don't attempt if yours has joint problems.) Ask your wolfdog to sit, then to lie down, then to sit again. Repeat. Getting up from a lying down position repeatedly is physically tiring!

Lupine Lookie-Loos

You might not find a trip to the post office or to put gas in your car very exciting. To your wolfdog, however, a car ride is a moving smorgasbord of fascinating smells, sights and sounds. If you're not able to take your wolfdog places because he has issues with other dogs or people (work on those issues separately), taking him along for short automotive outings is a great alternative. You can make those jaunts even more exciting by stopping at your local pet supply store to pick him up a treat along the way. Pack trips can be fun. Just don't get those fur-kids going on a singalong!

Vehicle Safety Note: Have a barrier between front and back seats, or crate your wolfdog. You don't want him in your lap when driving, or going through the windshield in the event of an accident. Never let your wolfdog ride in the back of a pickup truck unless he's crated and/or tethered; riding untethered can be fatal, and is also illegal in many states. When leaving your wolfdog in the car temporarily, be aware of temperature; leave windows slightly open. It takes only minutes for a canine to die in a hot vehicle. Take trips when it's cool and comfortable outside.

Let's Play A Game

What? Your wolfdog doesn't know any games besides Chew On The Human and Raid the Garbage? Here are a few new ones to try:

Find It In this game, you hide a toy and your wolfdog's mission is to find it. Begin by placing one of his favorite toys in plain sight. Get him excited about it. When he "finds" it (goes to it, even if it's two feet away from him), praise like crazy, then run to him and toss it for him a few times. Then "hide" it again. Gradually increase the hiding distance of the object. Next, make it harder by partially hiding it, i.e. leaving it peeking out from under a sofa cushion. Once your wolfdog is into the game, either put him in another room while you hide the object, or put him in a sit-stay facing away from you while you do so (you'll have to teach him not to peek, by stopping each time he does). Then release and let him go! Besides burning excess energy and engaging your wolfdog's mind, this game is also a wonderful outlet for that woofie predatory drive; there is the tracking of the "prey" and then the chase when you throw the toy for him.

Hide and Seek This is a great game that can be played indoors or out. It is also excellent for strengthening your wolfdog's recall. See *I Just Want Him To Come...* for rules.

The Name Game Teach your wolfdog the name of an object; for example, a ball. Place the ball in front of him. Each time he touches it with his nose, say "ball" *as* he touches it, then give him a treat. After a number of fast repetitions, begin to say "ball" just *before* he touches it. As canines learn at different rates, you may need to break this up over a few sessions. When he reliably responds to the verbal cue "ball" by touching the ball, move on to the next step. Put the ball and another object close to each other, and say "ball." He's got a one in two chance of getting it right. If he touches the ball, make a big deal and reward him. If not, say in a neutral tone, "Try again." (*Technical Training Tip: The "Try Again" is known as a No Reward Marker, or NRM.*) If he doesn't respond with another attempt, give the cue "Ball" again. Once your wolfdog gets really good at this game, make it more difficult by having him choose the correct object from a group of three.

As a more advanced version of this game, teach the names of three different objects (each in its own training session), then put them in a row and ask him to choose each one as you call them out. Your friends will think you have the smartest animal on the planet! You could even teach your fur-kid to retrieve each object and bring it to you. And just think, if you teach him to find and retrieve keys, you'll never have to worry about misplacing them again.

The Nose Knows What better game to play with an animal who can actually sniff out objects which are buried under snow, than scent discrimination? Wolfdogs are naturals! Scent discrimination games are similar to the Name Game, except here, your wolfdog chooses the correct object by determining which one has your scent on it. (See *Resources* for a beginner's book on scent discrimination.) Scent games are big fun in a grassy yard. Along with the Name Game, scent games are great to play indoors on rainy days, and useful too for wolfdogs who are not mobile, i.e. recovering from surgery, older or arthritic.

Agility

Okay, so maybe you've seen more Shelties than wolfdogs compete at agility trials. That doesn't mean these natural athletes aren't able to do it. After all, just picture the ease with which your wolfdog clears your six foot fence! Why not put all that grace and energy to good use leaping through tires and over jumps? To start, get yourself a beginner's book on agility (see *Resources*). Purchase used agility equipment (frequently seen on internet auction sites) or make your own. PVC pipe can be used to construct jumps, plungers double as weave poles, etc. Be creative. Or, join an agility class which uses positive training methods. Whether at home or in a class setting, the important thing is that your wolfdog will be using his mind to learn new tasks and will get great exercise running the course (as will you). Practicing agility will also make you a better trainer, and is a great way to have fun with your fur-kid.

This wolf-like dog enjoys agility!

While You're Away, The Wolfdog Will...Play?

So, great Woof-Parent that you are, you've made sure your fur-kid has lots of love, attention, and mental and physical stimulation. But what about when you're not around? Boredom often translates to trouble, and wolfdogs can get into an amazing amount of trouble in a short amount of time. If you're gone for long hours every day and can't get home for lunch, consider asking a friend to come by, or hire a dog-walker. Have them take your companion for a stroll or at least play with him for a while. This is especially important if he is an "only child."

That initial burst of "what can I get into" energy usually happens in the first half hour after the humans leave. So, let's give 'em something constructive to do during that time. Here are a few suggestions:

The Great Kibble Hunt This one is for one-wolfdog situations, or where multiple wolfdogs have no issues with each other over food. It is appropriate if you feed kibble; I wouldn't try it with raw meat. Measure out the kibble. Before you leave, instead of putting it in bowls, fling it all over the yard! Yep, you read that right. What will ensue is the Great Kibble Hunt. Hey, wolves hunt for their food, why shouldn't your fur-kid work a little? This is a fun and productive way to keep your wolfdog busy. He'll get rewarded as he finds each piece, and by the time he's done, he'll have that much less energy left to get into trouble.

Kongs In the *Kongs and Other Sanity Preservers* chapter, you'll find a treasure trove of information on how to stuff these magical balls. A well-stuffed Kong® can provide hours (or at least long, productive minutes) of Something To Do, as your wolfdog tries to get to the treats. Just think about all the things he's *not* getting into in the meantime. You can, as an alternative to the Great Kibble Hunt, stuff your wolfdog's kibble in the ball and leave it with him to work on when you're gone. If your wolfdog is not especially destructive, hide a Kong or two so that he first has to find them, then excavate.

Marrow Bones Beef bones that contain marrow on the inside and a bit of meat on the outside will keep your wolfdog busy for a long time. Buy them at the market and feed raw. They're healthy, too.

The Great Outdoors

Though the ideal situation is for your four-footed companion to be able to accompany you anywhere, the reality is that many people have wolfdogs who live in outdoor enclosures. Most of these are high content wolfdogs who are not well suited for in-home living. Some have been rescued, and have always lived in enclosures. This does not mean they can't have a wonderful quality of life, filled with lots of attention and stimulation.

Joell Severns runs *A Wolf Experience* in Reno, Nevada. The organization brings wolf/wolfdog education to the classroom and does rescue whenever possible. Here, Joell shares her thoughts on enhancing the lives of wolfdogs who live in outdoor enclosures:

"Wolfdogs love to chase each other in and around things, so providing an area of their enclosure to do this in will give hours of enjoyment. Straw bales, trees and large rocks are just a few of the things you can use as obstacles. A wooden platform that is high enough for them to run under but still jump on to is wonderful. It not only offers an area to chase each other under and to get shade, but it also offers a lookout point on which to lay and view their small kingdom and to play "King of the Hill." (Make sure the platform is not next to the fence line, as they could use it for escape.) To add a tunnel, build a box the length of the platform (large enough for them to crawl/run through), then secure it to the bottom at ground level. Another thing you could add is a tire swing—just add a few extra four-by-fours and secure the tire in a hanging position about two feet off the ground. (*See illustration.*)

Since all canines live by their sense of smell, a gift of something old, grimy and wretchedly stinky will thrill them to no end! Go to a nearby creek, stream, river or pond and find an old slimy stick to bring home for them. Sniff....Aaaaah....Ecstasy! That old sock that can stand on it's own? That's heaven to your friend! A dead fish might turn your stomach but not your fur kid's! And how about the cheapest, most vile bottle of perfume/cologne (you know, the stuff sold by the gallon) you were given as a gift? Just sprinkle a little on the ground and they'll roll for hours! (*Note: Another fun-to-roll-in option is cedar chips, which are pleasant-smelling to humans, too. - NW*) Tuna fish water, deer musk and other odor-attractive oils from the sporting good store work just as well. Also, every once in a while, go buy them a bag of steer manure or top soil and dump it in their pen.

Remember, the stinkier the gift, the better. Use your imagination. I discovered some of these things quite by accident. A fresh green pile of horse poop, a leather boot, an old slimy log, a hot pink tube of lipstick. (Believe me, there's nothing more comical than a punk-rocker wolf strutting down the road very proud of his new spiked do!)

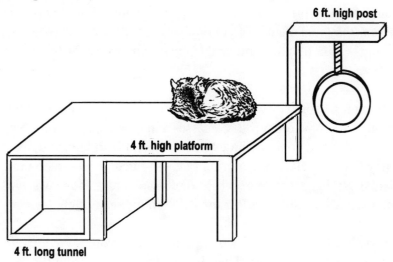

A Wolfy Jungle-Gym!

Another way you can please your fur kids is through their stomachs. When purchasing bones, I like to buy the whole cow leg bones. They last longer than cut marrow bones, and should keep them busy for a couple of days. I first wash them with 30% human grade hydrogen peroxide to kill any bacteria, then hand them out. The nice part about these bones is after a week I can take a hammer to them and split them open. Aha! Marrow is exposed and they become engrossed again.

Different seasons mean different treats. In the hot summer months, I fill plastic milk jugs half way with water and freeze them until they're slushy. Then I stir the slush, adding in bite-sized pieces of jerky or hot dog, fill the rest of the way with water, and let it freeze solid. It's a good way to keep them busy and well hydrated. Frozen rats from the pet store work as well. Try hiding them around their enclosure so your wolfies can "hunt" them up. (Actually, any treat they like will work with this method.)

Summer also brings watermelon, peaches and apples. Frozen or fresh, they make a cool treat on a hot day. If you feed peaches, split the fruit in half, remove the pit (peach pits can be toxic) and freeze.

Hunting season is one of my favorite times of the year, as I have many friends who share the carcasses of their kills. I get everything from meat and bones, to hides and feathers. (Warning: Neighbors may not appreciate that your fur kids use a deer head as a bowling ball!) Wild game is an excellent diet supplement; the new scents and sensations are great for mental stimulation as well.

In the late fall, I like to buy pumpkins for everyone. I cut the tops off and gut the innards. Then I place treats inside, put the tops back on, put them out in the yard and watch the fun. One time Lobo was so desperate to make sure he got one, he pushed his head inside and got it stuck. Feeling Bear nearby and afraid he would lose his prize, he took off running! Poor guy had to wait a few minutes for rescue so Mom could collect herself from the ground, where she'd fallen from laughing so hard! If only I'd had a video camera!

Finding things to entertain your wolfdogs isn't that hard. Just be sure what you give them is safe. Remember, the more you do for your animals to keep their minds' stimulated, the happier they are, and the less destructive they'll be. The end product is harmony for all. Be creative and have some fun!"

Fear Issues

Any canine, wolfdog or not, can be fearful. Wolfdogs in particular often seem to be more sensitive to stimuli than their non-lupine counterparts, and fear reactions may be more frequent and/or more intense. The word "skittish" is often used in wolfdog circles to describe a wolfdog who shows this type of sensitivity.

Early socialization to other canines, children, places and things can go a long way in preventing fear of those things later in life. But let's face it, not all of us have well socialized wolfdogs. Some are adult rescues; some have been abused; and some wolfdogs (especially high contents), despite all the best socialization in the world, still have fear issues.

The Face of Fear

Fear is a physiological, psychological and emotional reaction to a stimulus. A wolfdog who is fearful will exhibit specific body language which may include ears pulled back, head lowered and tail tucked. Additionally, he may yawn, lick his lips, or sniff the ground (see *Understanding Body Language and Signals*). Pacing can also be a sign of fear or anxiety. Strangely enough, fear can look a lot less like being afraid and a lot more like aggression. Understandably, many people mistake the former for the latter. For example, a wolfdog who snarls or barks at another animal may actually be afraid of that animal, and that posturing is his way of trying to get the animal to back off. A wolfdog who is truly afraid may also try to hide or flee the situation.

Never force your presence on, or pursue physical interaction with a fearful wolfdog. Besides making the fear worse, it can be dangerous to you. *Any animal who is afraid can be dangerous.*

For example, many people have been bitten by their wolfdogs while trying to load them into the car. The wolfdog was afraid, the human forced the issue, and a bite was the end result. A better approach is to diffuse the situation at that moment, then work on the cause of the problem when things aren't so stressful.

Who's Afraid of the Big Bad Human

If your wolfdog is afraid of you, a family member or visitors:

Don'ts:

- Don't hover over him. Wolfdogs are especially fearful of things overhead.
- Don't wear dark sunglasses or hats. Scary stuff to wolfdogs!
- Don't make fast movements or yell. (That also means don't yell at your kids or anyone else while your wolfdog is present.)
- Don't reach out for him. Allow him to approach and sniff you.

<u>Do</u>s:

- Crouch down, turn your body and face slightly away from your wolfdog. (Head-on is a more threatening posture.)
- With an extremely fearful wolfdog who you know to be no danger to you (i.e. a young pup), lay on the floor and let him approach.
- Keep your voice soothing, your movements slow and small.
- Let your wolfdog see that you have food treats, such as hot dogs. At any sign of him approaching, toss a treat (with a small motion) low to the ground, a bit away from you. Work toward gradually tossing them closer to you. Be patient. Do not toss treats if he shows fearfulness—you don't want to reward that behavior.
- Leave something with your scent on it, such as a t-shirt or sweatshirt you've just worn (or a towel you've carried under your arm) in the area your wolfdog rests in.

Some wolfdogs are afraid of one particular family member, often the man. If this is the case, the person he *is* comfortable with should sit in a room with the wolfdog. Every time the Scary Person enters, the Safe Person should start feeding the wolfdog treats, while acting relaxed and happy. When the Scary Person leaves, so does the food. The wolfdog will eventually come to associate the person with good things rather than with something to be afraid of. This is not a one-repetition quick fix exercise, but a process which should improve the relationship over time. (This classical conditioning approach can also be used to improve the association your wolfdog has with another canine member of the household.)

The Terrible Two—Things *Not* To Do

Two common mistakes people make when their wolfdog shows fear are to correct him or to reward him. Corrections usually happen when a wolfdog's fear is mistaken for aggression. For example, a wolfdog who is afraid of or not comfortable with other dogs may show it by snarling, growling or barking. This is often met with a jerk on the collar and a sharp verbal reprimand. That wolfdog now has another bad association with other dogs. He's probably thinking, *I knew they were bad news!* And so the problem worsens. And, if a wolfdog shows fear-based "aggressive" behavior which makes the other dog retreat, the behavior will become self-rewarding. After all, it worked. The Scary Thing went away! The proper way to handle this, if it does happen, is to (quietly and with as little fuss as possible) remove yourself and your wolfdog to a comfortable distance. This may necessitate taking him out of the area altogether. You would then, having learned that your wolfdog is not comfortable around other canines in that particular situation or at that close range, avoid it happening again as best you can, while work to desensitize him gradually to it. (More on desensitization in a moment.)

At the other end of the spectrum are people who inadvertently reward fearful behavior by cooing soothingly, "It's okay, don't be afraid." Those wolfdogs are getting rewarded by a soft, reassuring voice; some even get petted. Remember, a behavior which is rewarded is more likely to happen again. The proper thing to do if your wolfdog shows obvious fear is—nothing. Just stand there. You could even lighten the situation a bit by laughing, or saying in a light-hearted way, "Oh, silly, that's just the (insert scary stimulus here)!" You are conveying to your wolfdog that the pack leader isn't afraid of that silly thing, so he needn't be either.

A Little at a Time is Effective and Kind

A kind, effective way to address fear issues is desensitization. Desensitizing your wolfdog to whatever he's afraid of involves a very gradual increase in exposure to the stimulus (heretofore referred to by the highly technical term, "Scary Thing") at low, comfortable levels. Exposure is paired with positive rewards so that the wolfdog's perception of the Scary Thing changes to one of it being a Good Thing. (Yep, another hi-tech term.) As the wolfdog gets comfortable with the low level of exposure, the level is raised gradually over time, until the Scary Thing no longer elicits a fear response. Desensitization is not just for objects, canines or people that your wolfdog may be afraid of. Maybe your wolfdog has a fear of you clipping his nails. Or is he afraid of riding in the car? Does he freak out when you try to put a leash on him? All of these things, and many more, can be addressed by using desensitization techniques. One thing before we get started... Please realize that desensitization can be a very slow process. Patience is mandatory. Don't move through the steps too quickly, or you'll be back to square one.

So Far Away...

One important variable in desensitization is distance. In situations where objects, people or other dogs frighten your companion, begin with the Scary Thing at a distance. Just how much of a distance will depend on your particular wolfdog. While one wolfdog's comfort zone with children may be ten feet away, another may not be able to relax unless those kids are 50 feet away (and some days I know just how they feel!). Pay attention to your wolfdog's body language. Watch for stiffening of the body and calming signals (see *Understanding Body Language and Signals*). Begin at a distance at which your wolfdog feels comfortable. Simply stand in this "comfort zone" with him, feeding treats (if he's not too stressed to take them), keeping both of you relaxed. Remember, your own tension will be felt by your wolfdog, so breathe and stay calm. As he relaxes, move slightly closer to the Scary Thing, and continue to feed treats. Don't rush things. If your wolfdog knows Sit or other commands, or how to target (see *Clicker Training*), practice these things while you stand there. Giving him something to do will take his focus off the Scary Thing and get him more comfortable.

At each comfortable distance, reward. Move closer gradually, taking care not to push too far too fast. You will need to do many repetitions of this exercise. If your wolfdog makes ten feet of progress in one session, that's excellent! Go home and try again the next day, beginning at that ten-feet-closer distance. If your wolfdog begins to show signs of anxiety, you've gone too far too fast. Revise your program, go back to the comfort zone, and proceed more gradually.

What's That Sound?

Some wolfdogs are fearful of certain sounds. If the source of the sound has a volume control (i.e. a stereo), begin at a low level. Pair the giving of treats with the playing of the sound, raising the volume gradually as he becomes more comfortable with it. If there is no volume control (i.e. a vacuum cleaner), consider whether there is there some way to muffle the sound (i.e. closing the door to the room the object is in). If not, begin at a distance from it, gradually shortening that distance as your wolfdog becomes more comfortable. Remember to give lots of treats and remain calm yourself.

Keep in mind that canines associate things very quickly. Try to set it up so that nothing inadvertently scares your wolfdog while you're working on desensitization, or it could make them even more fearful of the Scary Thing. Case in point, here's what happened when I attempted to desensitize Soko to the Dreaded Microwave Beep (DMB): One day, seemingly out of the blue, Soko decided the beeping sound of the microwave was a Scary Thing. At first it was just the microwave. Then she figured out that the food that went into the microwave came from the freezer, so every time we opened the freezer door she ran out of the room. Then, because the freezer was in the kitchen, she wouldn't come near the kitchen. This was getting ridiculous! Finally, I enlisted my husband's help to set up a desensitization session. He stood by the microwave while I stood with Soko in the living room, approximately 30 feet away, yummy treats at the ready. The plan was, he would open and close the microwave door gently as I fed Soko hot dogs. As she relaxed and ate them, we would move slowly closer to the microwave. I would eventually, after she was comfortable with the door opening and closing, move on to address the DMB. Well, we never got that far. I started feeding hot dogs; but by accident, instead of closing the door gently, my husband slammed it shut. After that, Soko was afraid of hot dogs! (Not to worry, I put the hot dogs away and when I brought them out again a few weeks later, she was fine with them.) Remember, always be sure you have total control of the Scary Thing and as much control of the environment as possible. You wouldn't want to take a wolfdog who was afraid of children, for example, to a busy park. There's too much chance of a child running up and frightening him. Instead, you would enlist a friend with a calm, mature child who could stand a distance away and work with you slowly and safely.

Other Fears

There are many wolfdogs who are afraid of specific sounds that we don't have control over, such as thunderstorms. One solution to this is to get a recording of the sound, then play it constantly at a low level, eventually increasing the volume as your wolfdog gets comfortable with it. Of course, reproducing lightning, wind and a change in barometric pressure is nearly impossible. Still, if the noise is the main trigger for the fear, the recording/playback method may help.

Thunderstorm-phobic canines may also benefit from an over-the-counter hormone known as melatonin. Originally sold as an insomnia preventive for humans, melatonin has shown promise in calming canines who exhibit fear during thunderstorms. In investigating melatonin's effects, researcher Dr. Linda Aronson tried it with her own dog, with dramatic results. Her seven-year-old Bearded Collie, who usually urinated, tore through the house and dug at the carpets during thunderstorms, stayed awake and alert but remained calm. If your wolfdog is thunderstorm-phobic, speak to your veterinarian regarding melatonin. I would also strongly suggest getting a copy of the excellent article "Bring In Da Noise" Part 2 in the May 2000 issue of *Whole Dog Journal* (see *Resources*), which addresses the subject comprehensively.

Another common fear involves specific locations, especially when your wolfdog has had a bad experience there. The vet's office is a common example. Even when vets take care to make their patients calm and comfortable, they are still by necessity administering sharp needles and handling their charges in ways that can be perceived as frightening. If your vet's staff is willing to work with you, bring your wolfdog to the office for a friendly visit. Have the staff reward your woofer with treats (you can slip these to the staff when you walk in if they don't keep treats on hand) or petting, if he enjoys that. Be sure that when you go for an actual visit, the happy atmosphere prevails and *you* don't tense up, inadvertently signaling your wolfdog to do the same. If the uniform the vet wears that triggers your wolfdog's fear reaction, see if you can get a used version of the same uniform. Wear it while you play with your wolfdog and while you feed him treats. Try to recreate the experience of him being up on a table for exam at home too, pairing it with happy talk and rewards.

It's Only Natural - Remedies

Flower Power

In addition to desensitization, there are a few things which may aid your worried woofer on the road to becoming a calm canine. One is flower essences. The original and best known are the Bach Flower Remedies. These natural flower essences work on a vibrational level. Though just *how* they work is somewhat of a mystery, many pet owners report great results. All it takes is a few drops in your woofer's drinking water each day. The effect is subtle; your wolfdog will not have that glazed, drug-induced look. What will hopefully happen is that some of that anxiety *edge* will be gone, and your wolfdog will be calmer. A nice thing about flower essences is that they do not cause unfavorable reactions in combination with other medications. It is also impossible to overdose an animal on them. In other words, they may help, and at the very least, they won't hurt.

There are specific Bach remedies for specific situations. Rescue Remedy, the most popular for pets, is actually a combination of five different flower essences. There are other singular essences geared to specific needs. For example, mimulus works on fear of known things; rock rose, on extreme panic/terror; and aspen, on fear of unknown things. These remedies may be used for short-term situations (i.e., a thunderstorm) or longer ones such as adjusting to a new home. Rescue Remedy, along with the other Bach Flowers, were originally created for use by people and can be found at many health food stores. See *Resources* for an excellent book on using Bach Flowers for animals.

My Friend Herb

Herbalism is an ancient healing method that has enjoyed a surge in popularity in recent years. If you think about it, using herbal remedies on animals is perfectly natural. In the wild, sick animals instinctively seek out plants which contain the medicinal qualities that will heal them. People have used parts of plants for medicinal purposes for thousands of years. Why shouldn't our canine companions benefit from their healing qualities?

The herb valerian can be calming; slippery elm syrup may help diarrhea and vomiting; a tea made from alfalfa, white willow bark and burdock may help arthritis. As herbs contain healing ingredients in their natural form, they have none of the side effects associated with medical drugs. Most herbs are inexpensive, and while they may take a bit longer to work than traditional medicine, at least they're not doing harm. Check your local pet supply store for prepared herbal remedies, or learn to make your own (see *Natural Healing for Dogs & Cats* in *Resources*).

Of course, there are also prescription medications available for extremely fearful canines for whom herbs and flower essences just don't cut it. Consult with your veterinarian if this is the case with your wolfdog. Whichever remedy you choose, if you know a potentially frightening event is coming up, i.e. the Fourth of

July, do a trial run before the actual event. Gauge your wolfdog's reaction to the remedy. That way you can adjust the dosage, or try a different approach if necessary.

The Magic Touch

Tellington Touch (commonly known as Ttouch) is something that might not immediately come to mind as a tool to use with fearful canines, but it can be surprisingly helpful when dealing with fear issues. Ttouch is a form of hands-on massage, based on small, circular movements over the animal's skin. There are specific touches around the ears which can be particularly beneficial in allaying fear. Ttouch has been used in programs throughout the world on both domestic and exotic animals, with great success. There are books and videos available to show you how to do Ttouch with your canine (see *Resources*).

Though there are some fears which can be slow and/or difficult to work through, most can at least be lessened over time. Investigate the methods outlined in this chapter, and if necessary, consult a canine behaviorist for one on one help.

Guarding

Imagine this: One morning, you reach out to take a stray sock from your wolfdog, who has been helpful enough to find it. You've taken things from him many times before; only this time, hackles raise. The head lowers, eyes stare. A low growl issues forth. You don't need a Wolfdog-to-Human Dictionary to get the translation: "Back off, it's mine!" If your wolfdog has ever snarled, snapped or growled when you attempted to take something from him, you have experienced guarding behavior. Guarding of objects, food or even locations is collectively termed "resource guarding."

Resource guarding is fairly common and is completely natural. After all, for a wolf in the wild, that scrap of hard-won meat may well mean survival. If another wolf were to try to steal it away, you bet there would be a whole lotta snarling going on! Just because resource guarding is instinctive doesn't mean it's acceptable for your home to turn into *Wild Kingdom*. There are ways to stop these behaviors, and to prevent them from ever starting. Before we get to exactly how to do that, a word about growling...

Growling: Not All Bad

Some folks feel that growling is an unacceptable behavior which should be stopped at all costs. After all, an underling shouldn't be allowed to show such audacity to the pack leader, right? Wrong. That logic is faulty, and potentially dangerous. Look at it this way: Imagine that someone comes up to you on the street, grabs your purse or wallet, then just stands there with it. Most likely, a response such as "Hey, what're you doing?" (or something more colorful but less printable) would fly from your lips. Now imagine the same scenario, only you are mute. There is no way for you to communicate verbally. Wouldn't you grab for your possession? And if you were extremely stressed by the situation, isn't it possible that you would become physically violent? Think about it. If we take away our companion's natural way to warn us that he is uncomfortable with something, what options do we leave him? Many canines who have been taught not to growl progress to biting without warning. Those same canines often end up euthanized or given up to shelters, paying for a problem they didn't create.

If your wolfdog growls, try to figure out why. Are you touching him in an area which is physically sensitive? Is he in pain? (If a wolfdog who has never shown this tendency starts suddenly doing so, a veterinary visit may be in order to rule out physical ailment.) Is there perhaps a bone buried under the spot you're innocently standing on? Regardless of the reason, if your wolfdog is growling and guarding, the behavior needs to be addressed. *Do not, however, push it at the moment of his lupine power play*. Walk away, act disgusted, then address the cause of the behavior when things are calm. Remember, *responding to aggression with aggression only escalates the undesirable behavior.*

Object Guarding

Possessive wolfdogs live by the motto "What's mine is mine, and what's yours...is mine." Any toy, bone or goodie is fair game; possession is nine-tenths and then some with these guys! Some wolfdogs guard from people in general. Others guard from one specific family member, often the child. (Children are also often the first family member to discover this guarding tendency the hard way, so it is important to determine whether the behavior *is* actually person-specific, or whether the child simply noticed it first.)

C'mon, make my day...

Resource guarding is best solved with a two-part approach. One is to use specific exercises to discourage guarding behavior, and the other, to reinforce our status as leaders in the wolfdog's mind (see *Alpha*). If there are children involved, adults should progress through this entire program of exercises first. When all adults in the household have successfully completed them, the child may begin the sequence, under adult supervision.

I'll Swap Ya

In our purse or wallet-grabbing example, let's assume you still can't speak. But this time, when the person grabs your purse or wallet, they immediately stuff a twenty dollar bill in it and hand it back to you. *Wow, that's weird*, you'd think, relaxing a bit. My guess is that if they did the same thing five times in a row, by the fifth repetition you'd be handing that personal property over quicker than you can say, "Take my purse, please!" Using that same logic, we can teach wolfdogs that People Coming Near My Stuff Equals Good Things. Here are some exercises adapted from Jean Donaldson's "object exchanges," as outlined in her excellent book, *Dogs Are From Neptune* (see *Resources*):

First, determine what your wolfdog's absolute favorite toy or treat is. It can be something he has actually guarded, or is likely to. This is the Most Valuable Object. Then rank which toys or treats are a bit less valuable to him—ones he's not quite as crazy about. Lastly, which ones are Absolutely Boring?

Begin these exercises with an Absolutely Boring Object. It doesn't have to be a toy or treat. It can be a paper cup, for that matter. Have some Really Yummy Treats such as bits of cut up hot dog hidden on or near you. Don't show the treat first; you're not trying to bribe him. *One person should do this entire sequence before another begins*:

OBJECT EXCHANGES

1. Give the Absolutely Boring Object to your wolfdog.
   If he doesn't take it in his mouth, that's okay.
   Leave it on the floor in front of him.
2. Take it away, immediately presenting him with a
   Really Yummy Treat from your pocket.
3. Give the object back and begin again.

Repeat this exercise several times in a row. The aim is to have the giving up of objects become an automatic reflex. (If you'd like, after your wolfdog understands this game, you may add cues such as "Leave It" and "Take it.") After a few days, in addition to these repetitions, begin to do one exchange here and there throughout the day, in different locations and situations. Practice these exchanges over and over until your wolfdog is completely reliable with the Absolutely Boring Object. Then move on to something a little more exciting, working your way *gradually* up to the Most Valuable Object.

<u>Note:</u> *Until your wolfdog is absolutely reliable on object exchanges, use management to control the situation. For example, do not give your wolfdog a Most Valuable Object with your child in the room. And of course, never leave any small child unsupervised with any canine.*

Once one person has progressed up through the Most Valuable Object level, the next person can begin with the Absolutely Boring Object and work their way up. The second person will often progress more quickly than the first. *If the guarding is person-specific, that person should go last.* Realize that their progress may be slower. Once these exercises have been successfully worked through by all involved, do surprise exchanges now and then when your wolfdog has an object. Surprise exchanges should continue long after formal object exchange sessions have stopped. If they are not done now and then, the wolfdog may regress and the behavior may resurface.

Changing of the Guard

With high contents in particular, object guarding may be a difficult habit to break. If your wolfdog has grabbed something that you really need back, or is potentially dangerous to him, make a trade. Offer something else that he might be interested in, and when he drops the guarded object to take yours, pick it up.

85

Here is an amusing anecdote which involves guarding behavior in some of the pure wolves at Wolf Park in Indiana. Jill Porter relates *The Case of the Fuschia Frisbee*:

"One time a volunteer accidentally threw a fuschia-colored Frisbee into the wolf pen. Chinook quickly wrestled it away from the other wolves and proceeded to rip off small pieces. We were worried that he might get an intestinal blockage. When approached, he growled and bore his teeth down hard on the Frisbee, but when offered a hat, he dropped 'his' toy and trotted off with the hat. Then when offered a used Kleenex for the hat, he graciously accepted. We finally traded down to a small piece of meat for the Kleenex."

Sounds like a good deal to me! Here's another trading strategy success story from Jill:

"A few months later Chinook had in his mouth a bruised but otherwise uninjured bird, which had been caught by the wolves during a wolf-bison demonstration. Chinook proudly approached the audience with his prize and a woman in the audience screamed, 'It's still alive! Someone do something!' Dr. Klinghammer shouted for Pat and Monty to 'Do something.' Pat offered her hat and, somewhat reluctantly at first, Chinook dropped the bird. Pat's hat, in turn, was traded for a tissue. The bird, stressed and bruised, was rushed to a local rehabilitator. Surprisingly, it survived."

The moral of the story? If the trading strategy can coax an injured bird from the mouth of a pure wolf, it can certainly get an old, dirty sock away from your wolfdog.

Food Guarding

Many people, especially those with young children, feel it's safest to isolate their wolfdog at feeding time. If you have a rescue animal whose habits you are not yet familiar with, certainly, use every caution. But if you have a pup, or an adult wolfdog you have had for some time, the safer course is to get him accustomed to having people around while he eats. After all, it is very likely there will be a time when your wolfdog is eating and your child happens to walk by. Better to get your wolfdog used to their presence in a safe, progressive manner than to surprise your woofer and risk injury to your child.

Free-feeding (leaving food down all day) is a practice which can encourage food guarding from people and other canines. The wolfdog may become possessive of the food left in his bowl, the bowl itself, and/or the space around it. Feeding twice a day (for adults) and picking food bowls up after meals eliminates these possibilities.

Scheduled Feedings: Though you should certainly space feedings out, i.e. one morning and one late afternoon or early evening, avoid feeding at the exact same time each day. Vary mealtimes by as much as two to three hours. The reason for this is simple. Canines who are fed on a strict schedule become extremely stressed when that schedule is not adhered to. There will be times when you're unavoidably delayed in coming home, oversleep, etc. Getting your wolfdog used to a flexible schedule avoids stress for both of you. The less stress, the less chance of behavior issues.

87

With a pup or adult who does not show food-guarding tendencies, the whole family may perform the following guarding-preventive exercises. For safety's sake, adults should perform them first, and children should do them only when supervised:

1. Handle food in the dish while your wolfdog eats.
2. Approach as your wolfdog eats. Squat down next to him (without hovering over him), and place a Really Yummy Treat in his dish. He'll think, *People Coming Near My Stuff Equals Good Things!* Then nonchalantly go on your way. Children should walk by without squatting and drop the treat in the dish to begin with, then progress to squatting next to him.
3. Feed some meals by hand, a morsel at a time. This is also an excellent, pleasant method for teaching your wolfdog that all good things come from you, the pack leader.

If your wolfdog already guards his food:

1. If you are free-feeding, switch immediately to feeding twice daily. If your wolfdog doesn't eat after ten minutes, pick the bowl up. Put it away until the next feeding. It may take a few days for it to sink in that he can't graze all day, but no canine will starve itself. Don't give in or feel guilty. Pick up dishes after each meal.

2. Feed in different rooms of the house. Your wolfdog may have developed a possessive attitude about one certain spot or room; changing the scenery may help.

For these last two exercises, adults should be the only ones to participate until the behavior is absolutely under control. After that, children may carry them out, but only under strict supervision.

3. As your wolfdog eats, walk by nonchalantly, barely glancing over. From a safe distance, drop a really yummy treat in his bowl and keep walking.

4. If possible, hand-feed every meal, in a new location and without the presence of a bowl. This changes your wolfdog's attitude from one of food being a valuable thing he has to defend *against* you, to food being a valuable thing that comes *from* you. Of course, use your discretion with this last one. Do not put yourself in danger by trying to hand-feed a wolfdog who is apt to take a few fingers along with the kibble.

Note: Whether your wolfdog has ever displayed guarding behavior or not, children should be taught to never approach the wolfdog while he's eating without an adult present.

Location, Location, Location

He Who Controls The Resources Has The Power, and a wolfdog who blocks doorways or access to areas is living that creed. Location guarding is more subtle than object or food guarding, but is still potentially dangerous. Families with more than one canine often notice one blocking access in this manner from the other. That's fine. Let them sort it out between them, as long as no one gets hurt. But if your wolfdog is blocking access from you, especially if he snarls or growls when you try to walk by, you have a problem that needs addressing.

High-ranking wolves often give a subtle side-bump to lower-ranking pack members to move them out of the way. You can approximate this behavior if your wolfdog is standing across a doorway, or otherwise blocking your path, by gently bumping your hip against him as you walk by. Notice I said a gentle bump, not a harsh shove or kick. Good leaders are gentle. This movement sends a subtle signal to clear a path, the leader is coming through. For a few ideas on dealing with a wolfdog who is prone to guarding doorways, refer to the *Alpha* chapter, 8. "Control Access."

Whichever type of guarding your wolfdog displays, take heart. Though these behaviors can be downright frightening, with time and patience, they can be modified. If you don't feel comfortable doing the exercises on your own, especially if children are involved, consult a professional trainer who uses positive methods. And pat yourself on the back for caring enough to tackle the problem rather than giving the animal up. You're one of the good guys!

"Huh? You Talkin' To Me?"
Training Attention

Have you ever seen the movie *Taxi Driver*? Remember when
Robert DeNiro whirled around and said, "Huh? You talkin' to
me?" Do you really want your wolfdog to turn into a Doggie
DeNiro when called? Of course not! That's why training attention
is so important. Asking your wolfdog to "Come," "Sit" or
anything else is useless if you don't have his attention first.

The Face of Love...Or at least Treats

A fun and effective way to teach attention entails the use of the
clicker (see *Clicker Training*). If you prefer, substitute saying the
word "Yes!" in each spot the clicker is indicated. Either way, the
click or the "Yes!" works as a marker, to let your wolfdog know
that what he is doing at the exact second he hears the marker, is
what you want. Begin in an area with no distractions. If you live
in a home where there are kids running around, televisions blaring
and everything happening all the time, lock yourself in the
bathroom with your wolfdog. Bring along some well-hidden treats
and the clicker. Have a seat. Do nothing. Wait for your wolfdog
to look at you. When he does, click and treat. Do this each time
your wolfdog looks at you, without calling or otherwise luring
him. He should soon catch on and begin glancing at you more
frequently. Once he's "got it," move to another low-distraction
room in your house and start the exercise again. If you don't
have distractions in the house to begin with, the kitchen is a
wonderful room in which to start attention training. Ever notice
how our companions seem to find us endlessly fascinating when
we're in the vicinity of food?

After a few sessions, make the game a little harder. Hold the clicker in one hand, treat in the other. As your wolfdog watches, slowly extend the arm with the treat straight out to the side. Don't say a word. Your wolfdog will likely track the movement of the treat, then stare at it. Don't say a word and don't move. (That's the hard part!) He will eventually look at your face instead. The instant he does, click and treat. Vary holding the treat straight out, above your head, or anywhere else you can think of. (Just don't hold it too close to your wolfdog.) Once he is reliably looking at you each time you hold the treat out, add his name *just as he begins to look at you*. When he does, click! and treat. Once he's caught on, begin to say your wolfdog's name just after holding out the treat but *before* he looks at you. Don't forget to click and treat as he looks at you! Once he's got it, repeat this game in different locations.

You might assume that your wolfdog knows his name. Great. But does he respond *each and every time you say it*? With these simple exercises, you are conditioning the reflex to look at you automatically and reliably each time you say his name. Do five to ten rapid repetitions, then break for 30 seconds or so. Repeat. Keep training sessions for attention no longer than three to five minutes. Pups will have a shorter attention span than adults, so keep puppy sessions to two to three minutes. Practice these exercises throughout the day, progressing slowly to areas with more distractions. Work indoors, outdoors, and eventually with heavier distractions present like children and other dogs.

Loook Eeen to My Eyyys...

Once your wolfdog is reliable on these attention games, expect him to hold your gaze a little bit longer before clicking. It's okay to use verbal encouragement. As he looks, say his name, then say in a soothing voice, "Good boy watching me, good boy 2, good boy 3," then click and treat. By doing this you have some way of counting how long he's held your gaze, and you are encouraging him to keep doing so. Extend this time by small increments until your wolfdog will gaze at you for ten seconds.

"Huh? You talkin' to me?"

93

Always be sure when doing attention exercises that your eyes are soft and friendly, lids partially lowered, rather than hard and staring. A hard stare is a direct threat in the animal kingdom!

Try the "Find My Face" game: Make it a bit harder for your wolfdog to find your eyes, by turning your body slightly to the side when you call his name. He must walk around to find your face. When he does, click and treat. You may progress to facing completely away from him.

Once your companion is doing wonderfully on the previous exercise, call his name as you walk away from him. Again, he must find your face to earn the click and treat. This is a great way to teach your wolfdog to pay attention whether you are motionless or moving, and also sets the stage for loose leash-walking.

Take It On the Road

Now that you've got one fabulously focused fur-kid, take your act on the road. Is there a pet supply store in your neighborhood? Bring your wolfdog there. Keep the leash nice and loose, and stand back a comfortable distance from the people and dogs coming and going. You don't want the distractions to be too tempting. Click and treat whenever your wolfdog looks at you of his own volition. In a seperate exercise, call his name. As his eyes meet yours, click and treat. If you've done your homework, he may well respond to you calling his name even as another dog passes. Keep the reinforcement rate high (click-treat, click-treat, click-treat!) and the game interesting. If the situation proves too distracting, don't feel badly. It just means that you need more work in lower-level distraction areas first, or at a greater distance. Stick with it, and you will be rewarded with a wolfdog whose head virtually whips around when you call him. Who'da thought?

"I Just Want Him To Come When I Call Him!"

If I had a dollar for every time I've heard that phrase, I'd be e-mailing this manuscript from a beach in Tahiti. Oh, I can see you out there, slapping your thigh and laughing, "Come when I call him? Ha! I'm lucky he checks in when he's tired of digging up the yard!" Though some individuals definitely require more effort than others, the fact is that a reliable recall *can* be achieved, even with wolfdogs.

Why, you might ask, should you take the time to work on a reliable recall? Let me share this story... Years ago, my husband and I took Soko, our German Shepherd, to the beach. This particular beach runs right along a busy stretch of freeway in Southern California called the Pacific Coast Highway. We parked on the shoulder like everyone else. My husband opened the passenger, beach-side door of my little (pre-Jeep) Honda hatchback and bent to tie his shoelace. In a flash, Soko was over the back seat and out the door. She ran around the front of the car and headed out to the freeway. Heart in my throat, I leaped out of the car. My reflex was to run after her, but I caught myself. In my best training voice, I called, "Soko, Come!" and gave the hand signal, just as we'd practiced hundreds of times. Thank goodness, she turned and came right to me. Disaster averted. Soko is laying at my feet as I write this, and definitely gives Two Paws Up to a reliable recall!

Hopefully your wolfdog will never be in a life-or-death situation where the recall makes the difference. If it does happen to you, remember that in most cases chasing will only cause your wolfdog to run further; and in a foot-race, unless you've trained for the

Olympics lately, you're not likely to win. On a less dramatic note, with wolfdogs receiving all the bad press they do, a well-behaved wolfdog who responds when its owner calls is a good ambassador for wolfdogs everywhere. If you frequent dog parks or other places where dogs and owners gather, this is especially important. If it looks like your wolfdog is going to get into a scuffle with another dog (watch the body language), a well-timed recall can prevent an incident. No matter whose fault a dog fight might be, your wolfdog is always at risk if the other owner cries "wolf," especially if you live in a state where wolfdogs are illegal.

"Cookie" and Other Magical Words

Ever watch someone at the dog park trying to get their dog to come to them? "Come, Jake!" Pause. Nothing. "Come to Mommy, Jake, where's my good boy?" Still no Jake. Finally, "Jake, *Cookie!*" *Whoosh!* Jake appears, leaving a smoking trail behind him. Now, as far as I know, the word "cookie" has no special magical powers, though your wolfdog may beg to differ. The secret is that Jake has been conditioned from the start that the word "cookie" means a reward is coming. Every single time in his doggie life Jake's heard that word, something wonderful followed. Jake's no fool! Of course he comes running when he hears it. So why can't you condition another word to mean just as much as "cookie"? The answer is, you can.

Let's talk about the recall word. Most people use, "Come!" A perfectly good word, unless of course you've already been using it and it has come to mean as much to your wolfdog as "spatula." If that's the case, simply choose another word such as "Here!" The idea is, we're going to start from scratch to condition your wolfdog that each time he hears this wonderful, magical word, he's going to get rewarded.

For now, do not call your wolfdog to come to you unless you are doing an actual training session, or are in a situation where you know beyond a shadow of a doubt that your companion will come flying. Those situations might include you standing two feet away with a bowl of food, jangling the leash to go for a walk, or him already moving toward you. If you're not sure, think to yourself, "Would I bet $50 that he'll come when I call him?" If the answer is no, don't do it. If it's yes, be sure to take advantage of the opportunity to help condition the reflex by calling him to you. Over time, you will be able to increase the distance and level of distraction and still get a successful recall.

Don't Let "Come!" End the Fun

Consider this scenario: Lisa's wolfdog, Lakota, jumps the fence and starts doing lupine laps around the block. In a panic, Lisa runs after him. Out of breath, she finally stops, stamps her foot and demands furiously, "Lakota, come here!" Lakota stops, hangs his head and slowly walks toward her. Lisa grabs him, chastising, "Bad boy! What were you thinking?" Who knows what Lakota *was* thinking, but you can bet what he's thinking now sounds a lot like *Gee, I came when she called, why is she yelling at me?!* Chances are, Lakota won't be so quick to come the next time he's called, and who could blame him? *Never, ever call your wolfdog to you to punish him.* In this example Lisa could have tried running the other way, calling "Byeee Lakota..." or better yet, she could have used a pleasantly voiced recall, made a happy fuss when Lakota came to her, clipped on the leash, played with him a bit, then taken him home.

Be sure that coming to you when called never results in anything your wolfdog might consider negative. The Lakota scenario illustrates one negative outcome. Calling your wolfdog to come while he's playing with his canine buddies, then clipping on the leash and leaving would be another. (People do this at the dog park all the time!) Getting a bath is yet another unpleasant consequence for many dogs. If you need your wolfdog to be with you, fine. Go get him. Just *don't call him to you if he's not going to like the result*, especially during this training phase. You do not want your wolfdog to learn that "Come!" means the End of Fun Things For Wolfdogs. Once he understands the recall, if you let your wolfdog off-leash at the park, call him to you, give him a pet and a treat, then let him go play again. If, however, he does not come when you call *one time*, go to him, snap on the leash and leave immediately. *You* control the consequences of his coming to you and of his not coming as well.

Let's Get To It!

Recall training exercises should be started in an enclosed area with no distractions—just the happy trio of you, your wolfdog and some treats. Hide the treats in your pocket or on a shelf or counter, rather than waggling them at him. We want him to respond because you're calling him, not because you're bribing him. Stand a foot away from your wolfdog. Call his name, and when you're sure you've got his attention, call, "Come!" in an upbeat voice. Motion with your arm as though you're urging someone across the way to come on over. Odds are, he'll come. *As he starts moving toward you*, encourage him: "Good boy, that's it!" When he reaches you, pet, praise, then give him the treat. In fact, keep up the praise and petting for a full minute or more, dispensing another treat to him every three seconds. (The credit for this method goes to trainer John Rogerson, who suggests keeping up the petting/praising/3-second treat interval until ten treats have been given.) This teaches your wolfdog to enjoy staying with you, rather than coming, getting the treat, then running off. It also helps your wolfdog to associate the petting/ praise with the treats, which will make the praise more valuable, and therefore still effective once you cut back on treats. Make a point of scratching near and loosely holding your wolfdog's collar with one hand while treating with the other. This gets your wolfdog accustomed to you touching that area, so he will be less likely to take offense when you actually need to grab his collar. This method is especially helpful since many wolfdogs are neck-sensitive, as it sets up a good association with being touched in that area.

Note: The timing of the verbal encouragement as your wolfdog is coming toward you is crucial. Some canines, especially at a distance, will look toward you and may even start toward you, but veer away. Verbal encouragement helps keep them on track.

Now, I realize you might be thinking, *This is silly. Of course he's coming, I'm a foot away and have his favorite treat in my hand!* Exactly. Remember, we're starting with this tiny distance between you to set up the reflex that when your wolfdog hears that magical word, his body automatically begins to move toward you. In other words, *we're setting him up to succeed.*

Add distance in small increments. Graduate from working one foot away to two, then three and so on. If you're not sure when to add more distance, do two sets of ten repetitions. If your wolfdog comes to you successfully on at least eight of the ten in each set, increase the distance. If at any time he does not come to you when called, throw up your hands and say, "Oh well," show him the treat he would have gotten, and walk away. Try again in a minute. (On days when I'm feeling especially wicked, I'll even pretend to eat the treat myself.) Once your wolfdog understands this game and is coming to you reliably from ten feet away, move to another room with him and begin again, from a foot away. Always go back to shorter distances when you change location, as canines do not necessarily generalize a learned behavior to a new area. Practice in various rooms of the house, adding distractions gradually. Build on your successes. Progress to calling him from around a corner, from another room, from inside when he's in the back yard (with no distractions), then gradually add distractions. Raise the value of the treats as you ask for more difficult recalls. For example, while a recall from two feet away might earn him a piece of kibble or bit of dry cookie, a recall from the back yard while you're in the house, or away from play with another dog, would earn the best yummy treats you have, i.e. hot dogs or bits of cheese or chicken.

Some people prefer to use a metal whistle in addition to the verbal recall, or instead of it entirely. The advantage is that the whistle always sounds exactly the same, and the sound projects much further than the human voice. The obvious disadvantage is that you must have the whistle with you. Some people keep one on a key ring for this purpose.

Woofer In The Middle

Here's a fun game which strengthens the recall. Invite a few friends or family members to play. If you have only one other person handy, that's fine. Stand in a loose circle (or approximately ten feet apart, if there are only two people) with your wolfdog in the middle. Everyone has yummy treats handy, but hidden. The first person calls the wolfdog's name, then (assuming they have his attention) says, "Come!" in an upbeat, encouraging voice. As soon as the wolfdog starts toward them, they begin to verbally encourage him. When he reaches them, they reward with petting, praise, then a treat, while holding his collar gently. They should take care not to reach out or grab for him, but to let him come to them. They wait until he's done eating the treat. (If treats take more than a few seconds to eat, they are either too big or too hard.) The person who just treated the wolfdog then stands up and ignores him. The next person then calls him, and so on. Once your wolfdog catches on, you may find him looking around as if to say "Who wants me next?"

If your wolfdog knows "Sit," you may progress from expecting him to come to you, to coming to you and sitting. If you do add the sit, wait until he's sitting to lightly grasp his collar as you pet and treat.

Restrained Recalls

Restrained recalls make use of your wolfdog's *oppositional reflex.* This reflex causes canines, when pulled in one direction, to want to pull the opposite way. To perform restrained recalls, you'll need another person. Have them hold your wolfdog by the leash. Stand back a distance of ten feet or so and call your wolfdog, using your special recall word. Your helper should hold on to the leash a second or two after your wolfdog begins straining to get to you, so that he really wants to get there—then release. Encourage him verbally on his way to you. When he reaches you, give plenty of petting, praise and treats. If you call and he does not come to you after giving the recall word *one time*, throw up your hands and say "Oh well," making sure he sees the great treat he could have had. Trainer Leslie Nelson recommends this wonderful, wicked backup plan for when dogs don't respond on the first request: If you have another dog handy (a friend would be standing by with this dog), and your wolfdog has failed to respond to the recall, go over to that other dog and make a huge show of petting, praising, treating and even taking him for a short walk. Your wolfdog will most likely be quite upset by this. That's okay! In fact, that's the whole point. Have the first friend simply stand there holding your wolfdog's leash, not saying a word. In a few moments, try it again. Watch how fast he comes flying! *Controlling the consequences at both ends of the equation gives us control without resorting to aversive methods.* The wolfdog always has a choice, and presented with the alternatives in this way, will usually make the decision we want him to. Best of all, he thinks it was all his idea.

Hide and Seek

This is a fun game to play at home or in a safely enclosed outdoor area. Indoors, hide behind a couch, bed, dresser, around the corner of the room, or behind a door; anywhere your wolfdog can't see you. Outdoors, a tree, boulder or fence will do nicely. Don't make it too difficult at first. Call your wolfdog's name, peek to be sure you have his attention, then use your special recall word. When he finds you, make a big fuss, pet, praise, then give him a Really Yummy Treat, or surprise him with a tug or toss of a favorite toy. If you have another person with you, one of you can hold and distract your wolfdog while the other hides. Canines really enjoy this game, and it's another great way to strengthen the recall. The sheer fun of the game sets up yet another good association with that magical word!

Hiding and Seeking...   *...and finding a happy*
                                           Mom with yummy treats!

Where's The Proof?

Once your wolfdog is really reliable on the recall, proof it. Introduce distractions such as people walking by as you call him. Have kids run by. Get someone to walk a dog past you. Go from low-level distractions such as someone walking by at a distance, to high-level ones like someone standing nearby with yummy treats, dangling them in front of your wolfdog. Yes, it is possible to have such a good recall that your wolfdog will still come to you under these circumstances. It takes a lot of work, but it is definitely possible.

Work outdoors, at dog parks (a very high-level distraction area) and around strange noises and sights. The more effort you put into this, the more reliable your recall will be. And the more reliable your recall, the more others will see you as a responsible owner with a well-behaved, wonderful wolfdog.

Jumping and Digging and Chewing, Oh My!

Jumpin' Jack Flash

When I teach group classes for pet dogs, I hand out index cards the first night and ask my students to write down three behavior problems they'd like to see addressed. Inevitably, the answer that shows up most often is jumping up on people. Wolfdogs are as prone to this behavior as any other canine; but when a wolfdog jumps on someone, the problem can have more serious repercussions. Airborne wolfdogs can knock children (and small adults) flat without meaning to. Of course, so can many large canines. But while parents might be understanding about a Lassie look-alike knocking their child down in good-natured play, with wolfdogs, the unfortunate translation might be, "That animal mauled my child." While the animal in question may have done nothing wrong, these situations inevitably end badly for the four-legged defendant.

A wolfdog who is happy to see you can tear clothing and even skin. Being greeted shouldn't mean giving blood! On a less dramatic note, you might not mind your wolfdog jumping up on you when the weather is dry and you're in your "dog clothes." But what about when it's been raining, your yard is one big mud puddle, and you've just come home from a big night out? You sure don't need Timber's designer touch improving your wardrobe. Unless, of course, you prefer that chic pawprint pattern...

The reason canines jump on us in the first place is simple. They want our attention. Many people respond by pushing the offender off, while saying something like, "No! Get Down!" Let's examine that approach. Timber wanted to be spoken to and interacted with, so he jumped up. The person then not only spoke to him, but played this great pushing game every time he bounced back up. Hmm, do *you* think he's likely to do it again? Other non-effective methods include a knee to the chest or squeezing the poor woofer's paws. Those methods have something in common: They're unnecessary, not very pleasant for your wolfdog, and can actually be dangerous. I know of one woman whose exuberant German Shepherd mix came flying through the air to greet her. She raised her knee gently to his chest, as she had done so many times before. But this time, thanks to the dog's momentum, she actually broke two of his ribs. There are better ways. (Note: The fact that she'd done it "many times before" should have told her the method wasn't working.)

A full-bodied jump can knock down a child or small adult.

If safe, getting down to lupine level can make for a pleasant greeting.

Ignore the Boor

Here's how to stop jumping up quickly, painlessly and effectively:

Part One: When your wolfdog jumps up, fold your arms in front of you and make a quarter turn to the side. Look slightly up and away from him, as though you're snubbing him. Timber's efforts are now being answered by you turning into a statue. Not very interesting for him, is it. Some wolfdogs will, at this point, walk around in front of you. If yours does, just turn away again. Most will not keep this up for long. Whether he continues to jump or not, employ the second part of this plan, which is...

Part Two: Give him an alternate behavior to perform, then reward for it. If your wolfdog already knows Sit, ask him to do so. As soon as his rear hits the floor, reward with *calm* praise and petting, and if you'd like, a treat. If he jumps up again, turn back into a statue, then repeat the request to sit. If your wolfdog does not know Sit, or is too caught up in Flying Wolfdog Mode, wait until all four paws are on the ground (you'll have to be quick, this may last only a split-second), then reward. Repeat as many times as necessary. Remember, canines do what works for them, and wolfdogs are far from stupid. If jumping on you gets them nothing, but four-on-the-floor or sitting gets them what they want, they're going to choose the behavior which is rewarded.

Once your wolfdog understands the proper way to get your attention, set him up. Go out the front door, wait a few minutes, then come back in. If it seems your companion's lessons have fled his brain, begin again. Be patient. Once he's reliably *not* jumping, go back out the door and try again. Once he's consistently greeting you calmly without jumping, have someone else practice coming in the front door. Set that lovable bundle of fur up over and over, making sure he succeeds, praising lavishly as he does.

Remember, consistency is key when solving this behavior problem. If it's not okay to jump up, it's not okay—*ever*. If Timber jumps on you and is rewarded for it with petting or other attention, even every now and then, he'll continue to jump. Why wouldn't he? *Rewarding a behavior some of the time can actually strengthen it.* (Don't believe it? Go to a casino some time and watch people playing the slot machines.) Be sure all family members are on the same page about stopping the jumping. When dog-friendly folks come to visit, let them know you are working on this problem, and get them to participate in Timber's education. They'll probably be thrilled that you're doing something about it, and will be happy to do their part.

Chew on This

Chewing, as in chewing on inanimate objects, is a commonplace complaint of wolfdog owners. It is also a natural canine behavior. Pups chew when they're teething; canines of all ages explore the world with their mouths; and most of all, chewing is fun! The thing is, wolves are incredibly strong animals, with twice the jaw pressure of German Shepherds (1500 pounds per square inch vs. 750). They have great physical strength and energy. So when a wolfdog gets to chewing, the damage is often more extensive and severe than when, say, a Pomeranian has an attack of the nibbles. The Pom might inflict tiny tears in your couch, but you might well be able to scowl at your wolfdog through the hole he's chewed through the middle of it.

There are products on the market which are intended to discourage chewing. *Bitter Apple®* is probably the best known. The idea is that this bad-tasting stuff, sprayed on whatever the woofer is chewing, will deter him from chewing it again. The problem is, 15% or so of canines actually *like* the taste. I know; I live with one. Also, in many cases you'd need a vat of the stuff to cover all the things the wolfdog is chewing on. As far as taste deterrents, some people have used Tabasco sauce with success. Not too many canines like the taste, though there are some who remain unfazed by it. (*"Can I get a little more hot sauce for these wood chips, please?"*)

A better solution is to manage the situation. That means keeping things out of reach of your canine's canines whenever possible. It also means supervising your wolfdog when you are around, and redirecting the chewing to acceptable objects. So keep him within your sight. If he begins to chew on a forbidden object, say "No" or give a sharp "Eh-Eh!" then immediately give him a proper, legal chewie to work on instead. Praise as he chews on the acceptable object.

This may seem obvious, but be sure legal chewies are more appealing than the couch. Things that we think will entice might not be all that appealing to your wolfdog. A well-stuffed Kong® or juicy marrow bone should do nicely and will keep him busy for a while. Another tempting legal chewie is compressed rawhide. Ask the staff at your local pet supply shop to show you the difference between regular and compressed rawhide. The light-yellowish type, usually shaped like a bone with knots at both ends, can be unsafe. As pieces are chewed, gummy strands are pulled off and swallowed, and may lodge in the throat or intestinal tract. Compressed rawhide flakes apart instead. Stay away too from small, flimsy rubber toys which can be easily shredded, especially ones that squeak. Squeakers can be dangerous if ingested. (Why do I have this image of a large wolfdog trying to howl, but squeaking instead?) Lastly, don't let your wolfdog chew on articles of clothing. He won't distinguish between that old sock with the hole in it and the brand new one you left on the floor.

If, despite your best efforts, your wolfdog refuses to acknowledge your "Eh-Eh!" and redirecting-of-chewies, continuing to chew on the forbidden object, use a phrase such as a disappointed, "You blew it" and calmly remove him from the area. Ignore him for a few minutes, thereby giving him a "time out."

Whenever you are unable to supervise your wolfdog, i.e. he's in the house but you need to take a shower and don't feel like company, put him in a crate or other safe containment, or put him outside. The more carefully you manage the situation, the faster chewing will cease to be a problem. Keep in mind too that pups go through a teething stage that starts at around four months of age. As their baby teeth loosen, soon to be replaced by adult teeth, those adorable pups turn into chewing machines. The good news is, the teething stage ends at around seven months. The intensity of the chewing naturally decreases somewhat after that. In the meantime, chewing relieves teething pain, so give your pup a wet washcloth that's been put in the freezer. It will not only relieve his pain, but will also keep him busy, thereby lowering your stress level. (Naturally, you'll want to be present to remove the washcloth once it unfreezes and becomes a potential shred-toy.)

If your wolfdog is kept outdoors when you're not at home, be sure he has plenty of things to chew on, i.e. stuffed Kongs or marrow bones. Keep garden hoses and anything else you value out of reach. And don't forget, whether your wolfdog has been kept indoors or out, if you come home to find something that has been destroyed, it's too late for reprimands. Your fur-kid won't associate your anger with what might have been done hours before. Calmly clean up the mess and chalk it up as a reminder that *you* need to be more careful next time!

Exercise is an extremely important part of managing behavior. Whether the problem is chewing, digging, general destruction or a host of other things, burning off some of that excess energy through exercise and mental stimulation will help to lower the intensity of the behavior.

Can Ya Dig It?

Digging is another natural, instinctive canine behavior. Be that as it may, you don't want your flower beds dug up, or your yard to resemble the surface of the moon. So how do we stop it? The first step is to determine the cause.

Some wolfdogs dig "dens" in order to have a cool place to hang out. If you think this might be the case with your fur-kid, provide an alternative. Make sure he has plenty of shade, including a crate or doghouse as refuge. Hook up a misting system if possible.

Some dig to escape the confinement of a yard. These determined diggers usually tunnel right along fence lines, trying to get under and out. One solution to this type of digging is to bury a skirting of chain link approximately three feet wide, a foot or two down, all along the fence line. Wire the skirting to your existing chain link, then cover with dirt. If you have a wooden fence, drill holes at the bottom to attach the chain link skirting. If you don't want to go the chain link route and your wolfdog is not the Hulk type,

111

try placing some large, heavy bricks all along the fenceline. Your wolfdog will quickly learn that attempts to dig under are futile.

An alternative that will keep your wolfdog away from the fence altogether is electrified wire, or "hot wire." Stakes are set a few feet apart and run parallel to the fenceline, about a foot in. Wire is then threaded through these stakes, and runs chest-level to the wolfdog. The wire connects to a charger, which runs on either batteries or electricity. A ground pole completes the setup (for specific instructions refer to *Living with Wolfdogs*.) The wire is quite visible to the wolfdog. Most learn quickly that touching it results in a small electrical shock. Self-contained systems such as Fido Shock are easy to set up, inexpensive, and are available through pet supply stores. *(Note: An electric wire does not take the place of proper fencing, but acts as an adjunct to it.)* Some people feel that Fido Shock does not deliver a strong enough charge to deter their particular wolfdog. These folks opt to use a "cattle charger," which delivers a stronger, pulsating charge instead. Again, with either of these hot-wire options, the wolfdog clearly sees the wire and chooses to avoid it, eliminating the possibility of digging along the fenceline. This is not to be confused with "invisible fencing" systems, which deliver a shock to your wolfdog via a collar around his neck when he touches the invisible perimeter. *I do not recommend invisible fence systems.* In fact, I would rather avoid any relationship at all between electrical shocks and canines; but if it will ultimately save your wolfdog's life, I would use Fido Shock or another hot-wire system.

Since digging is a natural behavior, rather than trying to eliminate it, provide an appropriate outlet for it. Is there an area of your yard that could be designated Dakota's Dig-Pit? Have someone hold Dakota, or otherwise restrain her so she can watch what you're doing. Take a bone or favorite toy and bury it in the dig-pit. Release Dakota. She will probably, like any self-respecting canine, rush right over to investigate. Praise like crazy as she sniffs and digs up the buried treasure! Repeat this exercise at various times, then begin to bury yummy surprises in the dig-pit in secret. The idea is that digging in that particular area could yield great things at any time! When you see Dakota digging in an off-limits area, say "No" or "Eh-Eh!" then bring or call her over to the dig-pit, and praise her if she digs there instead. If you don't have an area that would make an appropriate dig-pit, you could use a large heavy rubber tub, or a child's wading pool filled with sand or dirt.

For small holes around the yard, try dropping some of your wolfdog's feces in, then filling the hole with dirt. That usually stops the digging at those particular sites. A friend of mine with a particularly tenacious wolfdog buried a water-balloon at the one spot her wolfdog kept digging in. It burst, spraying the woofer in the face, and he never dug there again. While I wouldn't recommend this as a first line of defense, in that particular case, it worked as a last resort. And remember, if you find holes which have already been dug, it's too late to reprimand.

Nipping: Help for Human Chew Toys

It's no fun to be a human chew toy, especially when the chewer has razor-like teeth and an endless supply of energy. Nipping and mouthing are, you guessed it, natural canine behaviors. Puppies explore the world with their mouths. When very young pups wrestle, play and mouth each other, they let each other know when the mouthing gets too hard. This is accomplished through sharp, high-pitched yelping; the offending pup backs off. That's how pups learn "bite inhibition," or just how hard they can bite down without hurting others. Bite inhibition is a useful thing for pups to know, especially when human skin is involved!

That puppy instinct to back off when they hear a yelp is hard-wired, so let's make use of it. Next time your pup bites down on you too hard, give a short, high-pitched, puppy-like squeal. If you've got the sound right, your pup should not only remove his teeth from you, but may look downright baffled. *"So sorry! I had no idea that hurt!"* For pups who do not respond to the squeal (or for human males who refuse to make that silly squeaky sound), try the "Eh-Eh!" as a way to back them off. It may not work for the same reason, but it may still work. Now comes the tricky part: You've got his teeth off you temporarily, but he's still got all that puppy energy. If you don't give him something else to do, and fast, he's most likely going to come right back at you with his teeth. That brings us to the second part of this particular solution, the "Lick-Lick Trick." Take a small dab of peanut butter and smear it on the back of your hand. With a closed fist, present the back of your hand to your pup. *As* he begins to lick the peanut butter and not before, say "lick-lick" in a high, happy voice. After a second or two, take your hand away and put it behind your back. Then present it again, repeating the exercise. You can get in a lot of repetitions this way, thereby strengthening the pup's association between the action of licking and the verbal cue, "lick-lick." (If your pup doesn't like peanut butter, try cream cheese instead, or even plain yogurt.)

Practice "lick-lick" at various times throughout the day. You can get children involved in this one, especially if the kids have been frightened by this little bundle of energy's nipping. It gives them a safe way to interact with the pup, and gets the pup used to hearing the "lick-lick" cue coming from the child. It also allows the child to feel he has some control over the situation. Naturally, any child-pup interactions should be done under strict adult supervision.

Strengthen the association of the words with the behavior by saying "lick-lick" any time your pup happens to lick you. Once he truly understands and responds to this cue, when he becomes nippy, give the high-pitched squeal. When he backs off, immediately present the back of your hand and say "lick-lick." He should begin licking instead. *Note: I once had a woman report that when trying the lick-lick technique, her adult wolfdog actually bit her. There is no reason a well-adjusted canine should bite you when presented with something yummy to lick, unless there are other problems to begin with. Please use common sense when using any of these techniques.*

Another effective method to lessen nipping behavior is the time out. As with chewing, when your pup begins nipping, say in a sad, disgusted voice, "You blew it." Or, use another phrase if you'd like, but be consistent about using the same words and tone of voice each time. *Immediately after saying the phrase*, bring your pup to his crate and put him in it. There's no need to shove or to add words like "Bad boy." You've already let him know with the "You blew it" that what he just did (nipped you) is the reason he's going in the crate. If you do it this way consistently, he will learn by association that nipping means the end of playtime. Leave him in the crate and walk away. If he whines or cries, ignore it. Once he's settled down, wait another few minutes, then let him out.

There is an old adage in dog training that the crate should never be used as punishment. While I agree, I think of it this way: When I was a kid, my bedroom was my refuge from the world. I would listen to music, lose myself in books, and generally felt safe there. My room was also where I got sent whenever my parents felt I was getting to be too much to deal with (okay, so I wasn't the perfect child). Did I then start having a bad association with my room? Heck, no! *As long as there is a good association to begin with*, being sent to one's room, or crate, is not going to change that association.

In the best of all worlds, one method for stopping a problem behavior would be effective for every canine. Unfortunately, it doesn't work that way. Though "lick-lick" might work like a charm with one wolfdog, it might have no effect on another. With that in mind, here are some alternatives for dealing with nipping:

- For children, be sure there is a toy, stuffed animal or some other object handy which they can get between them and the wolfdog. Instruct them that if the pup starts putting teeth on them, to put the toy in his mouth. (If you have an adult wolfdog who has severe nipping/mouthing problems, I would reconsider having him around children at all.)

- Redirect his attention. All that energy's got to go somewhere. See if you can get your pup involved in chasing a ball or playing with a toy, or do a brief training session instead.

- Be aware of your own mannerisms. If your pup is excitable, you need to be calm. Pulling your hands away and flapping them around only encourages more mouthing. Folding your arms in front of you and becoming very still encourages calmness.

For adult wolfdogs, start out with the methods outlined above. Always exercise extreme caution with a seriously pushy, dominant-type adult wolfdog. For example, I wouldn't advise squealing with an individual like that, though teaching lick-lick might be useful on its own. Know your animal and use your best judgment. For adult wolfdogs, a good method to begin with is time outs. After all, being deprived of your company is the worst thing that can happen to most wolfdogs. Just be careful when getting him into the crate.

As you may have guessed by now, I'm not in favor of forceful or punishment-based methods. But if all else fails, *and you feel you can do this safely* (i.e. this is not an unfamiliar adult rescue), place your hand, palm down, over the top of your wolfdog's muzzle, and curl your fingers gently around it. Scowl and say in a deep, growly voice, "No bite." If this has no effect, use the same motion, but this time, push the top lip down and under on one side so that it's wrapped around the top canine tooth. If your wolfdog bites down, he will bite his own lip. *Ouch!* Notice that *you* are not pressing down or hurting him; you are calmly holding the lip in place. He is making the choice.

The good news is, most pups outgrow nipping as they get older. And, if they're already adults and still nipping, most can be trained to stop. As with all behavior modification, the key is consistency. Hang in there!

Kongs and Other Sanity Preservers

Many complaints about "problem behaviors" in wolfdogs stem from an excess of canine energy, boredom, or a combination of both. Digging, chewing on objects, barking, self-mutilation and general destruction come immediately to mind. Some wolfdogs get especially wound up when their human pack leaders leave, and destruction usually follows within the first half hour. The solution? Give 'em lots of exercise and mental stimulation whether you're present or not.

What's considered adequate exercise by most of us, such as a brisk walk, barely ripples the surface of a wolfdog's energy reservoir! Physical exercise should include running off-leash in a safe, enclosed area. (See *Enrichment* for more ideas on physical exercise.) As far as mental stimulation, training is invaluable. You might be surprised just how much even a short training session wears your wolfdog out, especially if you are using methods such as clicker training where your companion has to figure things out for himself. (Remember that thirty minutes of exercise versus thirty minutes of calculus!)

Okay, so you're a great Woof-Mom or Dad who provides mental and physical stimulation on a regular basis. Great! Your wolfdog is that much less likely to do things you won't like. But to really set them up for success, let's give them plenty of stimulation when left alone as well...

Kongs are King

I am in no way connected with the folks who make the Kong[®], but I should be. I so believe in the power of these wonderful, magical balls that I should represent the company. I always tell my group classes, "Kongs will save your life"—and I'm not entirely kidding. At the least, they'll go a long way toward preserving your sanity. These extremely hard rubber balls have a tiny hole on top and a large one on the bottom. The magical thing about them is not that they bounce strangely when thrown (although that's fun too), but that when stuffed with treats, they become a yummy excavation project that will keep your wolfdog busy for a long while.

A wolfdog who is left with a well-stuffed Kong® may not even raise his head to say "See ya, don't forget to send a postcard!" as you leave; the presence of a stuffed Kong® can make all the difference to a wolfdog who needs to be crated; and a wolfdog in the sway of a Kong-induced trance is unlikely to be tearing up your furniture or other valuables. How long will this tasty trance last? That all depends on how well you've stuffed the ball, and of course, on your particular wolfdog. I've seen canines go through Kongs in five minutes flat, while others patiently try to get at the stuff inside for close to an hour.

Note: Though Kongs are very tough, the black even more so than the red, do not leave your wolfdog unattended with one until you are absolutely sure he won't shred it. Though most canines can not shred these balls, some wolfdogs most likely could.

Meal-in-a-Kong

For high-energy wolfdogs, feed meals in the Kong®. This allows them to work for their food and burn off excess energy all at once. After all, no one handed their lupine ancestors bowls of kibble way out in the wilderness! Here's how to do it:

1. Block the small hole at the top. This can be done with any soft, moldable treat, a bit of freeze dried liver, peanut butter or cheese.
2. Flip the ball over so that the big hole is now on top. Measure out the kibble. Fill 2/3 of the cavity with kibble, adding in some bits of hot dogs or cheese if you'd like. Pour excess kibble in bowl.
3. Fill the last third of the cavity with canned food, or kibble mixed with food roll, peanut butter or cream cheese. (Alternately, you could mix kibble and canned food and spoon the mixture in, or alternate layers of kibble and canned food.) This ensures that the kibble will not fall out too easily.
4. Place ball in dish, and serve.

Once your wolfdog has the hang of food excavation, make it more challenging. You might mix cream cheese or peanut butter in with the kibble near the bottom, to make it tougher to get out. You could also stuff a quarter of a piece of bread over the top of everything, molding it so that your wolfdog will have a harder time getting to the hidden treasures. I do this with Mojo, a confirmed Kongaholic, and believe me, he can still get to the goodies inside.

Suggestions from the Kong® Company

- Mix cheese pieces or cheese spread with kibble and microwave for 90 seconds. This creates a crust that sticks everything inside together. Cool before serving. *(Use a cup to contain ball when freezing or microwaving.)*

- Try various combinations of canned food, gravy, noodles, rice and mashed potatoes mixed with kibble, and freeze. Kongsicles!

- Plug the small hole with peanut butter. Turn it upside down in a cup. Fill ball with water, chicken broth or fruit juice and freeze. Another yummy Kongsicle! *(Frozen Kongsicles recommended for outdoor use.)*

Here are some other ideas (from various sources):

Simple: Stuff with dog cookies. Squeeze the large opening so it elongates, stuff cookies in. The cookies should be just big enough to fit through the elongated hole, but not fall out when the hole springs back into shape.

Fresh or Frozen: Block the small hole. Flip ball over. Mix plain yogurt with kibble, then spoon the mixture in. Serve as is, or freeze it for Yummy Frozen Yogurt Treats!

Hidden: Hide stuffed Kongs inside and outdoors. First your wolfdog has to find the Kongs, and will then stay busy getting the stuffing out. (Note: Use caution when hiding Kongs with a wolfdog who might shred your house to find them.) By the way, this form of hide-and-seek is useful for woofers who suffer from mild "separation anxiety," as it keeps them busy right after their person leaves.

Loading the ball with a meal and then placing it on top of the leftover kibble in a dish is a great solution for wolfdogs who eat too fast, or who attempt to inhale their food and then someone else's. Naturally, I have to do this with Mojo. Not only was he "wolfing" his food, but he would then try to get Soko's. The result of the above-mentioned solution is that first Mojo is slowed down by having to eat around the ball, then he has to work to get the food out of the ball itself. In the meantime, Soko is enjoying her food without Land Shark trying to snarf it.

No Bones About It

To say it's hard to find chewies that will keep a wolfdog busy for long periods of time is an understatement—but it can be done. Another great option in this regard is marrow bones, often labeled "Bones for Soup" at your local market. Marrow bones are also excellent for cleaning your wolfdog's teeth. Feed them raw. Butchers will usually cut them to size if asked nicely. A good-sized marrow bone should keep your wolfdog busy for a half hour to an hour. Peace and quiet. Aaah!

The Great Rag Wrap

If you're going to be gone for a while, here's a fun way to keep your wolfdog occupied: Wrap cookies, kibble or other treats in a rag, then knot the top. Wrap that rag in another rag and knot, and so on. What you'll end up with is the equivalent of a gift wrapped in one box, then a bigger one, and so on. The unwrapping alone is enough to keep your wolfdog busy, but if you want to take it one step further, hide the rag-wrapped treat. The first few times you do this, let him see you put it, say, in a shrub, or under his dog bed. Say "Find the treats!" and let him go. Gradually make it a bit harder, to the point where your wolfdog must find the well-hidden rag ball first, then unwrap it. Again, use caution. Don't make the game *too* difficult, or you might come home to a house that's been torn apart by one very persistent player.

Food Cubes and Balls

The most popular food cube on the market is the Buster Cube®. The idea is similar to the Kong®, in that your wolfdog must work to get to the hidden treats or kibble. There are four chambers inside the cube and a hole on top. Pour kibble in the hole, then shake to distribute it throughout the chambers. Your wolfdog must then paw and roll the cube for the kibble to fall out. This is not as simple as it sounds, and there is even an adjustment to make it more difficult. Similar products are also available, some of which are shaped like a ball rather than a cube. Know your wolfdog and consider whether this is the toy for him. If he's likely to put his mouth around the entire cube and crush it, this may not be your best bet. If, on the other hand, he's the type to paw and puzzle it out, you may have found another great option for burning off energy and keeping that sharp mind engaged.

Though each of the above-mentioned "sanity-preservers" take some effort on your part, think of it as an investment. The more you put into it, the more you'll reap the rewards of a better-behaved woofer, and some well-deserved peace of mind.

Loose Leash Walking

"Who's taking who for a walk?!" If that describes you and your wolfdog out for a stroll, don't despair. Pulling on leash is a common complaint of owners of large-breed canines of all types. For wolfdog owners, getting their canine companion to walk without pulling can be an especially tough challenge, as wolfdogs are usually large and be incredibly strong. Add to that the fact that Malamutes and Huskies, the two breeds wolfdogs are most commonly mixed, with are bred to pull and you've got one major drag! Though these factors can make things a bit tougher, take heart. We are not striving for a perfect competition heel. What we do want, and can definitely accomplish, is for your wolfdog to walk nicely in the general vicinity of your side, leash slack, without you looking like you're water-skiing on pavement.

Don't Be a Jerk!

Traditional methods of teaching loose leash-walking entailed putting a choke chain on a dog, attaching the leash, then taking off. Any time the dog forged ahead or otherwise left the owner's side, *pop!* The owner jerked the leash, the choke chain tightened, and if the collar was on correctly, loosened again. In other words, the owner waited for the dog to make a mistake, then corrected him. So the dog got information about what was *not* appropriate behavior, but there were no hints as to what he *was* expected to do. And while we're on the subject of physically manipulating dogs, let's not forget that pesky *oppositional reflex*, which basically means that if something pulls them, they want to pull against it. So here we come, with our leash, choke chain and smug assurance that we're in control. If the dog gets to the end of the leash and stays there, causing the aptly named choke chain to tighten, it's a standoff. They want to lunge forward against the

125

pressure of being held back, and we're holding on for dear life. Not very pleasant for anyone. Not surprisingly, many dogs never improve with this method.

Many owners argue that their dogs don't lunge "when the choke chain is on." That's probably a valid assessment, since the dog has most likely become so fearful of a jerking correction that he doesn't dare pull. Naturally, this stresses the dog the entire time the chain is on. And what about when it's not on? Wouldn't you rather have a canine companion who understands what you want and happily complies regardless of what training equipment happens to be on him at the time (or with no equipment at all), than one who complies out of fear of punishment? For a sensitive dog, as many wolfdogs are, a choke chain can do serious psychological as well as physical damage, not to mention the toll punishment-based methods take on your relationship.

Note: There is a metal collar known as the *prong* or *pinch* collar. I do not generally advocate its use. It is interesting, however, that a "properly used" prong collar, although it looks like an instrument of torture, is actually less damaging physically than a choke chain. So if the sight of a prong collar gives you pause, good! Now seriously reconsider the use of the choke chain, which can cause worse damage.

Turid Rugaas, author of *Calming Signals*, tells a wonderful story about strolling down the streets of an unfamiliar city, arm in arm with a friend. Each time the friend turns a corner or makes an unforeseen move, she either bumps into Turid or pulls her along. Turid uses this example to illustrate what going for a walk might be like for a dog who doesn't know what the rules are. Do you think it would it be fun to go for a walk in this manner? Would *you* want to make a habit of it? Now, what if this friend communicated with you as you went along, telling you when a turn or change was coming up? Wouldn't the walk go more smoothly and be a lot more fun for both of you?

If you have the opportunity to train your wolfdog to walk nicely on leash from puppyhood, great! Teaching proper leash-walking early on puts you way ahead of the game. If your wolfdog is an adult, or a pup who is already accustomed to pulling on leash, re-training him to walk nicely on a loose leash will take some work, but is definitely possible. Before we begin, consider this: Does your wolfdog pay attention to you when asked? If not, proceed to chapter H (*"Huh? You Talkin' To Me?"*) and practice the attention exercises as long as necessary before moving on to actual leash-walking.

Pack Leaders, meet the *Gentle Leader*®

If we're not using choke chains, you're probably thinking, *what are we going to use?* That depends on your particular wolfdog. If you're starting with a young pup, a flat nylon buckle collar will do just fine. That's right, just the plain ol' everyday collar he wears anyway. If you have a confirmed adult puller on your hands, you might want to consider a head halter. The Halti brand head-halter has been around for years. It buckles around the neck, with an attached piece that fits over the dog's muzzle, and a metal ring underneath to attach the leash to. Ever see a horse being led? That's a head halter. Trust me, if it can move a two-ton horse, it can move your wolfdog.

In recent years, a head halter called the *Gentle Leader*® has gained popularity. The design is similar to the Halti, but the fit is better. The Halti is one pre-sewn piece, which is fine as long as it fits your wolfdog's muzzle well; otherwise it can chafe, or he may be able to back out of it. The GL's muzzle strips are a separate, adjustable feature. It also buckles behind the dog's ears, rather than around his neck. GLs are currently available through professional dog trainers and veterinarians (although at the time of this printing, one popular pet store chain is beginning to carry them). The GL should be fitted and introduced to the dog properly, which is best done with the assistance of a professional trainer, or at the least, by watching the GL video or reading the literature.

Properly fitted, the GL allows a wolfdog to
open his mouth, drink water and howl!

The Gentle Leader® is absolutely not meant to be used with leash-pop corrections. As head halters direct the canine by maneuvering the head and neck, a harsh physical correction could result in injury. With a GL, the dog is never allowed to lunge to the end of the leash. As soon as he starts to move out ahead, a gentle pulling maneuver brings his head around so he is actually looking at the owner. It's a pretty nifty way to redirect movement and attention in one, wouldn't you say?

Though most canines adjust to the head halter fairly easily, there may be an adjustment period. On the first few sessions, your wolfdog might try to paw it off, rub his face on the ground to get it off, or in extreme cases, buck like a stallion. This will pass. Think back to how uncomfortable you were the first time you wore glasses, or a brassiere. You might not have liked it, but after a short while, you didn't even notice it was there. (Note: A small number of dogs become absolutely dejected with the GL on. There is a difference between this reaction and a simple adjustment period. I do not recommend the GL for dogs who become morose, as wearing it then becomes a punishment.) Some people are worried that head halters are sometimes mistaken for muzzles by neighbors and passersby. My feeling is, since head halters shift you instantly from manual to power steering, and are much preferable to choke chains, these are minor considerations. As for the neighbors, they should be thrilled that you care enough to train your companion. One trainer I know of sewed tiny embroidered flowers on her GL and the comments went from, "Is that a muzzle?" to, "Isn't that darling?"

Note: Head halters are not meant as an alternative to training, but as an adjunct to it. Some owners wean their canines off the GL on to a flat buckle collar, while others use it indefinitely. You are the best judge of your own physical capacity and your wolfdog's strength and behavior. Do what works for you.

We're going to approach loose-leash walking with a few different techniques. These are not intended to be taught as a sequence; each stands alone. As no one method works for every canine, try them out and use whichever one or combination of methods works for your particular wolfdog. Always begin in an area where there are no distractions, treats at the ready.

Follow the Leader

The first thing we're going to do is get your wolfdog to follow you. That's the whole idea, right? But being the sneaky trainers that we are, we're going to walk *backward* at first. Canines are more likely to follow when we move backward while facing them, so let's make use of that. If you are working in an indoor or safely enclosed area, lose the leash completely. If not, use a leash of five to six feet, and clip it to your belt loop. You won't be giving any corrections or holding the leash tightly for any of these exercises. (Timber: *Wow, I like this better already!*) Be sure there are no obstacles behind you. Face your wolfdog. Get his attention, then begin to walk backward in a straight line. The treats should be hidden in your pocket or bait bag. *As he follows*, quickly pull out a treat and give it to him. It is important to reward *as* you are both moving. This takes a little coordination, but we want to communicate to your wolfdog that following you is what is getting rewarded. In the unlikely event that your wolfdog will not follow you, try verbally coaxing him, walking faster, and if necessary, using the food as a lure by holding it by your side. Be sure too that he's not distracted by anything in the environment.

Once your wolfdog is consistently following you in this manner, add in some forward-walking. Take a few steps backward, then smoothly switch to walking forward, so that he ends up at your side at the completion of the turn. If you want your wolfdog to walk on your left side, when you make the switch to forward walking, turn right, in toward him. This will position him on your left. *Be sure to reward quickly and repeatedly when he is in the correct position, as you move along.* Keep the forward segments short so that your wolfdog is successfully staying by your side and doesn't have a chance to pull out front. Congratulations! You've begun to lay a solid foundation for loose-leash walking.

Note: If your wolfdog lags while walking on leash, be sure you are not applying pressure, thereby triggering his oppositional reflex. Keep the leash loose and try to coax him forward. Be happy and silly, not stern. Use food treats as a lure if necessary. When you do reward, hold the treat a bit ahead of him so he has to walk forward to get it. If he's lagging out of fear of the environment or something ahead, address that problem separately from leashwork, and for now, go practice in an area which is more comfortable for him.

Round and Round We Go...

This next one can be practiced off-leash, or, if you are working in an unenclosed area, with a 15-20 foot long line. As always, try to have minimal distractions. Start by strolling around the area, giving no commands, paying no attention to your wolfdog. At some point (usually very quickly) your wolfdog will follow you, naturally falling into heel position by your side. *As soon as this happens*, (click if you're using a clicker, then) reward him with treats and praise. If he continues to follow, keep the (clicks,) treats and praise coming rapidly. If he wanders off, ignore him and keep walking. To make yourself more interesting, try walking more quickly, switch off walking backward and forward, do whatever it takes to get his interest—but do *not* call him over. Your wolfdog will soon learn that walking by your side is the most rewarding thing he can do. Why *wouldn't* he do something he gets rewarded for?

Keep it Loose

Now let's snap the six-foot leash on. Tired after all those backward walks and turns? You'll appreciate this one. Hold the leash. Don't move and don't say a word. When there is slack in the leash (meaning he's not straining against it causing it to go tight), reward him. If you are clicker training, click at the moment the leash goes slack, then treat. When he pulls, causing the leash to go tight, do nothing. Stand still and don't say a word. When the leash goes slack again, (click and) reward. Your timing is crucial, as the leash may go slack for only a second at first. You'll find that after a few repetitions, your wolfdog will understand and the leash will become slack for longer periods. Good! We want him to learn that a slack leash is what we want, and more importantly, what *he* wants.

Slack leash + head halter = enjoyable walk!

Be A Tree

Now that your canine companion is clued in to the loose leash game, let's take him for a test drive. Set him up to succeed by starting in a low distraction area such as your living room or hallway. Encourage him to follow as you start walking by saying,

"Let's Go," "Follow" or whatever word you will consistently use, in an upbeat tone of voice. If he follows, great! Quickly reward him with a treat as you move. If he begins to lunge ahead (this will almost certainly happen at some point), *stop*. Don't move. Become as still and quiet as a tree. When the leash becomes slack again, say "Good boy" and resume walking. (Note: Your fur-kid should not get a treat when returning to proper position after a lunge, because many clever canines figure out that lunging/returning will earn them a treat. Instead, the continuation of the walk is the reward. The only time Timber gets a treat is when he walks by your side with the leash loose.)

Outdoors, if your fur-buddy drifts into Wolfdog La La Land while at the end of the leash, zoning out on the scent of a squirrel or something equally fascinating, get his attention by making a noise such as kissing or clucking. Or, pat your leg. You might also try stomping your feet in place with quick, tiny stomps. I get good results with that last one—I suspect it works because the woofer thinks you're leaving. When he responds, continue. Whatever you do, *do not stand there repeatedly calling his name*. The last thing we want is to is start having his name go in one ear and out the other, and become meaningless. After all, we don't want to undo all that good attention work you've done!

Being a tree can be frustrating, especially at the beginning. You might not get five feet before having to stop, and you will stop often. You may have started as a sturdy Oak but now feel more like a Weeping Willow. Hang in there. Some wolfdogs catch on a lot quicker than others. To keep yourself motivated and to measure your progress, count how many times you stop over a set distance. Did you stop 50 times between your home and the end of the road? Fine. Now keep track and watch that number decrease. You may end up stopping an average of only 35 times the next week, and eventually work down to less than five. It's encouraging to track your improvement.

Above all, the rule is, *never allow the pulling to be successful.* Ever! Don't let Timber drag you over to that post so he can urinate, thinking it's okay because "We haven't really started training yet." *Any time your wolfdog is on leash, you're training.* Remember those slot machines, which work on a schedule of random reinforcement. Money might pour out after the fifth try—or the fiftieth. The point is, if it happens once, you'll likely try for a long time before giving up on getting that reward again. If your wolfdog gets rewarded every now and then for pulling, you can bet he'll keep trying because hey, it worked that one time. So be a sturdy, reliable Oak. It's well worth the effort.

A Word About Rewards

You will not have to carry food treats forever (though rewarding intermittently once the behavior has been learned is certainly helpful). Besides, what many canines find most rewarding on walks is to sniff and investigate! Use this to your advantage. If you have a wolfdog who is more interested in the environment than he is in treats, get a few good steps of slack leash walking in. Then, instead of treating, give the release word and run with him (so he's not pulling) to a scintillating sniff spot. Let him sniff for a moment, then say "Let's Go" and take off walking again. An alternate reward would be to pull out a tug toy, have a quick game of tug, then continue the walk. Walks should be fun and interesting for you and your wolfdog, rather than a boring training drill. Frequent rewards keep everybody happy.

Follow Me!

This is similar to the Be a Tree method, except now, when your wolfdog begins to move out ahead, instead of being a tree, you will walk in the opposite direction. There is no yanking or popping of the leash, but rather a slow, subtle pressure as you pull your wolfdog's head around toward you. (This is especially easy to accomplish when using a Gentle Leader®.) Note that you are not waiting until your wolfdog hits the end of the leash to begin your turn. Begin your turning movement *as soon as your wolfdog begins moving out ahead*, so that his turnaround is smooth. Once he sees that you are moving away, he's likely to follow. If necessary, take a few backward steps first to get him focused on following you, then turn forward. Be a good trainer and seize the opportunity to reward him as he moves into the correct position.

Look Who's Walking

Wolfdogs, like other canines, are apt to get distracted on walks. And when wolfdogs see things like cats zooming by, they get a *lot* distracted. Many also react to dogs behind fences, who are performing the ever-popular Territorial Bark Tango. So what to do when your four-footed darling goes from peaceful follower to fur-covered missile? Hang on—literally. Stand firm. Don't jerk, don't pull. Say, "Let's Go" in an upbeat voice and walk the other way. Dogs who get "corrected" by yanking and yelling each time they see another dog come to associate other dogs with this painful and frightening correction, which only exacerbates the problem.

Half the battle in relaxed leash-walking is looking ahead so that *you* see the cat, dog or other "trigger" before your wolfdog does. Get into the habit of scanning the path ahead. If you know where other dogs live, all the better. As you near one of these Bark Tango Palaces, get your wolfdog's attention. Baby-talk him, feed treats, do whatever is necessary. (If clicker training, and you've taught him to target a stick or the back of your hand, get his attention with some targeting.) Keep it up as you pass. With daily practice, the lunging behavior should decrease. After all, you've given your wolfdog a great, rewarding alternative to reacting to other dogs. (This technique also works for a cat or other stray animal. If possible, steer clear altogether. If not, keep your wolfdog's attention until the animal is out of range.)

Don't expect that your wolfdog will learn to walk nicely on leash overnight; it's a process. Start slowly with minimal distractions, and build gradually on your successes. Think of your daily walk as a training session. If you don't get further than the end of the block, that's fine. It *will* get better in time, and your efforts will pay off in walks that will be much more pleasant for you both.

Management

Training means working with your wolfdog so that he responds to your cues for particular behaviors, and behaves in ways that are acceptable to you. *Management* means setting things up so that he doesn't get into trouble in the first place.

Limited Access and Time Outs

Some behavioral problems are more easily solved by management than by training. Let's say you have a prized collection of wolf figurines. These fragile pieces of art reside on a bedroom shelf which is not quite out of your wolfdog's reach. (Then again, what is?) Do you spend days and weeks training him to stay away from them? Or perhaps train him to stay out of the room altogether? Here's a much quicker and more effective solution: Close the door! I know it sounds simple. It is! Does Timber raid the garbage? Get a metal, heavy-lidded spring-top can, or place something heavy on top of the lid. Sure, you could train your wolfdog to stop those behaviors, but so many problems can be avoided altogether with a little forethought on our part.

"Mmm, thanks for the great toy!"

Limiting access is a valuable management tool. Access can be limited not only by closing doors, but by closing off areas with tall, sturdy baby gates, or by putting your wolfdog outdoors or in a crate when you can't supervise. Another useful management tool is the *time out*. Time outs are wonderful for when your wolfdog gets into a frenzy of jumping, mouthing, racing around and being generally obnoxious. A time out can diffuse a situation before it escalates. It also avoids confrontation and any temptation on our part to use punishment.

Sturdy baby gates help with wolfdog pups and some adults.

A time out can take place in a crate, puppy pen, your yard, or any other safely enclosed area. *A time out is not a punishment*, but more of a cooling-off period. What we want your wolfdog to realize is that when he gets too wound up, all the fun stops; so, as he's doing his Deranged Energizer Bunny imitation, use a verbal marker such as a disappointed-sounding, "Time out" or "You blew it," then calmly bring him to the time-out area.

Keep 'Em Busy!

Giving your wolfdog something to do is a management tool. Why? Because by doing so, you are preventing him from doing all sorts of other things he can't possibly be doing at the same time. Stuffed Kongs and marrow bones are two great options. A well-stuffed Kong® goes a long way, and marrow bones are one of the few chewies that will keep a strong-jawed wolfdog busy for a long time. Those expensive chewies from the pet supply store don't last a tenth as long as the inexpensive, healthier marrow bones from the market. So next time you want a bit of peace and quiet, or you're having guests over and don't want Timber underfoot all evening, give him something to do that will make everyone happy.

Crates are Great

Crates, besides being a wonderful place for time outs, are an excellent management tool. While your wolfdog is crated, he can't be having a housebreaking accident; getting into the garbage; shredding things; jumping on counters; or a host of other undesirable things. Let's face it, no matter how vigilant our supervision, there are just some times when we're not able to keep up. Unless you bring your wolfdog with you into the bathroom (and I know people who do), he needs to be safely confined while out of your sight.

Here's a real-life example of the value of crates as management tools: One night my wonderful, ever-alert German Shepherd began barking at something outside at 4:00 a.m. My dogs have indoor/outdoor access at night, and at first, it didn't worry me. I figured there was a coyote or an especially bold rabbit out there. But as the nights passed and Soko continued to bark at 4:00 a.m.,

I realized it had become a pattern. Perhaps a neighbor's alarm went off at that ungodly hour; I don't know. Whatever the reason, it was not acceptable, especially as Mom can't get back to sleep once I'm up! At that point, some people would have gone for the bark (shock) collar. But why? Let's manage the situation instead. Out from storage came Soko's extra-large crate. She had been crate trained from puppyhood and always loved her "den." We brought it inside, and that first night when I said "In your house" (our puppyhood cue for her to go into the crate), she went in without a peep. She's been sleeping happily (and *quietly*) inside it ever since. And, I'm happy to report, I can now sleep through the night. Management is a beautiful thing!

More Management Magic

You may not think of exercise as a management tool, but it is. Remember, management is setting the situation up so that the wolfdog doesn't get into trouble in the first place. A well exercised wolfdog is much less likely to get into trouble, as all that energy has found an appropriate outlet. A wonderful mantra is "A tired wolfdog is a good wolfdog." (For specific exercise suggestions, see *Enrichment*.)

Management takes many forms. A woman wrote to me recently that she couldn't seem to get her wolfdog trained. It seemed that when she'd leave meat on the kichen counter, he'd jump up and eat it. (Imagine that.) "He's meat crazy!" she wrote, obviously distressed. Well, I don't know about you, but my guys would snarf meat or anything else that tantalizing if I left it on my kitchen counter in about half a second. Sure, you could put a whole lot of time and effort into training your wolfdog to stay away from food on the counter when you're not there. But isn't it easier to just *put it away*? In my house, food that needs to sit for a moment while we're out of the room gets put on top of the refrigerator. Putting a baby lock on your cabinets or fridge will prevent your wolfdog from getting into them; locking the gate will prevent your gardener or kids from accidentally letting your wolfdog out; making sure your fencing is adequate will prevent potential tragedy. It's easy. It works. So think ahead, and set the stage for success. A whole lot of trouble can be prevented with just a little bit of management!

"No, They Won't Turn on You"... and Other Responses to Persistent Myths

As certain myths about wolfdogs seem to crop up time and again, I thought a little dispelling might be in order. Here are the most common, along with the real low-down:

"They'll turn on you."

Unless you slam your wolfdog's tail in the car door or similarly hurt/surprise him (in which case his snapping at you would be justified), it is very unlikely that he will "turn on you." Wait, let me modify that. If you've been physically abusing or training your wolfdog with harsh methods, he may let you know one day in no uncertain terms that he is not now nor has he ever been happy with the arrangement. That could certainly look like "turning on you," though I couldn't say as I'd blame him.

What *will* happen is that your wolfdog will grow from a pup into a mature adult. If you have not taken the time to train him and to establish leadership from the get-go, you may have a canine on your hands who will challenge you for dominance. (See *Dominance Challenges and Other Not-So-Fun Stuff.*) This type of challenge is sometimes mistaken for one's wolfdog "turning on" them. Dominance challenges, by the way, are not the exclusive domain of wolves and wolfdogs. Any breed of dog may challenge their owner. It is, however, a tad more frightening to be challenged by an adult wolfdog than, say, a Miniature Poodle.

143

"They never bark."

Actually, wolfdogs can and do bark. The misconception is that high content wolfdogs and pure wolves bark just like dogs. High contents and pures may utter a low, chuffing, warning type of bark, but it's not the same as a repetitive, loud, doggie-like bark.

Lower and mid-content wolfdogs may or may not bark like dogs. There is also some anecdotal evidence that wolfdogs who do not usually bark may demonstrate barking as a learned behavior, when living with other canines who do so.

"They're untrainable."

You can probably guess my answer to that one. Obviously, they're trainable. What *doesn't* work well with most canines and with wolfdogs in particular are harsh training methods. Using punishment-based techniques may well result in a wolfdog who loses trust in you, and who might even injure you. Employing positive training methods, on the other hand, will earn you a wolfdog who is not only well trained, but one who enjoys training and respects you as leader.

Higher contents and pure wolves will likely take more effort to train, and the responses may not be as consistent as with low-to-mid contents or dogs. Regardless of the amount of wolf content, there is no reason to use "they're untrainable" as an excuse for not taking the time to train your own wolfdog to the best of your ability.

"They howl at the full moon."

Okay, this one isn't entirely untrue. Sure, they howl at the full moon. Heck, I've been known to do that myself! (Unlike me, however, they seem to have perfect pitch.) Truth be known, they also howl at the crescent moon, the half moon and the dark of the moon. It may be that because there is more light during the full phase of the moon, there is more activity and therefore more to howl at. What *is* true is that wolves are *crepuscular*, meaning they are most active at dawn and dusk; so they are generally inclined to howl most often during those times, regardless of the moon phase. They also howl more often during breeding season, which takes place during late January and February.

Wolfdogs A-Z

"They make excellent watchdogs."

Oh, they'll watch all right—from under the bed as someone walks off with your stereo. Wolfdogs are most often mixed with Husky or Malamute. Neither of those breeds are meant to guard or alert. Combine that with the fact that wolves are naturally afraid of people, and you've got some pretty poor guard/watchdogs (especially high content wolfdogs). Sure, it's possible that a wolf mixed with a lot of, say, German Shepherd could be a watchdog. Then again, if that's your goal, why not get a German Shepherd?

"They can't live in the house."

Sure they can. Plenty of low contents and some mid content wolfdogs live in the house. Many higher content wolfdogs start out in the house and end up outdoors; some wolfdogs prefer it that way. Whether your wolfdog shares your home is a question of what you are willing to live with.

A high content wolfdog may be harder to housebreak than a doggie-dog. Also, many wolfdogs are destructive in the house. I have heard first-hand stories of wolfdogs eating through drywall, shredding couches and tearing up linoleum. People who live with high contents indoors have usually made some concessions in their lifestyle. Of course, wolfdogs are not all like this, and proper exercise will go a long way towards taking the edge off some of that destructo energy. Whatever the wolf content, I don't know of many wolfdog owners who leave their four-footed darlings in the house unattended for any length of time.

146

"They'll kill children."/"They're great with children."

The sad fact is that dogs of just about every breed have killed children. Many of those deaths could have been prevented by proper containment of the animal and/or supervision of both animal and child. *Children should never be left unsupervised with any canine, wolfdog or not.* I have seen pure wolves stalk children through the fence at Wolf Park in Indiana. As the wolves follow the kids back and forth, the parents comment on how cute it is. It's not. I have seen wolfdogs in private ownership show predatory behavior toward children. I have also seen wolfdogs playing nicely with children, everyone obviously having fun. It is my personal feeling that wolfdogs do not belong in homes with small children. A lot of doggie-dogs don't either. We can not say across the board that all wolfdogs will injure children, nor that all wolfdogs are great with children. We do know that wolves have a well developed prey drive, and that prey drive is triggered by movement and sounds such as crying. In my opinion, in a home with children, that should be given careful consideration. In the end, it all boils down to knowing your particular animal, training both wolfdog and child on proper interactions, and never, ever leaving them together unsupervised.

"He doesn't know whether he's wolf or dog."

This one in particular drives me crazy. It is usually followed closely by, "The wolf part is battling the dog part." I can't tell you how many times I've heard otherwise intelligent people use that as the reason they believe wolfdogs are "unpredictable"—as though these animals are in a perpetual state of existential angst, agonizing over what species they are. *Hmm, the dog part of me wants to play with that bunny, but my wolfy instincts tell me to kill it. Whatever shall I do?* I don't think so. The cold, hard truth is that, "He's unpredictable" often translates to "He's had no training," "He's undersocialized," or "I have no clue how to read canine body language." The dog is not the one who's confused here. It would benefit us all to become well versed in canine body language, learn positive training techniques, and give our woofers lots of love and the best care we can. I don't think an animal given those things will have any identity crisis. Do you?

"Off" (or "Leave It")

"Off" or "Leave It" cues your wolfdog to drop or back off whatever's in or near his mouth at the time. It can be used in situations where you need to get something back from him (i.e. a toy or bone), to remove his mouth from someone's shoelaces (or arm for that matter), or to ignore something on the ground while out for a walk.

Be careful about which word or phrase you choose. If you usually say "Off" when your wolfdog jumps up on furniture or countertops, use "Leave It" for this new behavior instead. Using the same verbal cue for two different behaviors is confusing to your wolfdog. As always, be sure that everyone in the family is consistent about which word applies to which behavior.

Back Off, Balto!

To teach "Off," hold a dry cookie in your closed fist. Let it peek out just enough from the hidey-hole formed by your curled index finger and thumb that your wolfdog can sniff and even lick at it, but not actually grab it. Keep a yummy treat hidden in your other hand, behind your back. Let your wolfdog get interested in the cookie. Be careful not to pull your hand back as he explores. (If he's too rough, yelp "Ouch!" Move the cookie out of sight, wait a moment, then continue.) Let him explore. The *moment* he pulls back, even for a second, say "Yes!" (or click if you are clicker training), then quickly reward with a treat. Note that when we reward, we do not give the cookie he's been sniffing, but rather, a treat from the other hand. The reason is that the cookie he's sniffing will eventually translate to your sock, a toy, or some other item you don't want him to have. We don't want him thinking, *If I back off this thing, I get to have it.* Do five to ten repetitions of this exercise at each training session. Your wolfdog should pull back further and faster as he understands the exercise. Once he does, add the verbal cue "Off" or "Leave It" *as* he pulls back. Gradually increase the time you want him to stay back before you give the reward. You can eventually require him to back off and sit. (If he is absolutely too rough with his mouth to wait for him to back off on his own, use the verbal cue *first* to back him off, then reward.)

1. Let him get interested in the cookie

2. Wait for him to pull back

3. Reward from the other hand

The Street Beat

Another application of "Off" is to have your wolfdog leave objects on the floor or street alone. For this exercise, place the cookie on the floor, making sure he sees it, then quickly cover it with your shoe (taking care not to bear down and crush it). Your wolfdog will sniff and try to get at the cookie. Say "Off," then click or say "Yes" when he backs off. Don't forget the treat!

The Chair Dare

Once your wolfdog's response to "Off" is reliable, take it a step further. Put the cookie on a chair in plain view. Stand next to it. When he approaches the cookie, say "Off." If he continues his approach, quickly cover the cookie with your hand and start over. If he leaves the cookie, reward him with a treat. This can also be done without a chair, by placing the cookie on the floor and quickly covering with your foot if he goes for it. You'll need to be quick for this one, or all your wolfdog will learn is that the silly human isn't as fast as he is! Once he gets good at this, use it for those times he decides to go counter-surfing.

Child's Play

If you have children, work with them so they are able to tell the wolfdog "Off" or "Leave It." This gives them an alternative to attempting to remove things from the wolfdog's mouth themselves, which can prove dangerous. (Of course, children should be supervised during all training sessions.) "Off" also comes in handy for another common behavioral problem that often involves kids—nipping at pants legs or hanging hems. Pups especially are prone to doing this. Someone walks or runs by and the pup begins grabbing at the pants leg with his teeth. Many people, especially children, tend to react by pulling away and walking off, or running faster. What a great game for the pup! Instead, have them stand still, fold their arms and say "Off," praising when your pup backs off. Continue this until he gets the idea that grabbing pants legs makes all the fun stop. You might also consider avoiding clothing with hanging hems until the pup is better trained.

Generalize Those Jaws

Once "Off" is completely reliable using the cookie, practice with other interesting objects, in your hand and on the floor. Use it when you take walks. Just about any canine will sniff at things on walks, often discovering unsavory tidbits we'd rather they didn't touch, roll in or ingest. Use "Off" in those situations, rewarding your wolfdog with a treat, petting and praise, or a short, fun sprint or game when he backs off. Remember that it may take some time for him to generalize "Off" to different environments and situations.

Principles of Positive Training

Many methods of dog training advocate the use of harsh physical corrections. While dogs trained with these techniques may appear obedient, they are actually complying out of fear of punishment. It would be like someone putting a gun to your head and demanding that you do the Hokey-Pokey. Sure you'd do it, but is that what it's all about?

Aversive methods seemingly give the human immediate control, but have serious long-term repercussions. Punishment-based training causes stress and frustration, which often surfaces later as aggression or other behavioral problems. It teaches your companion to dislike training and to fear making a wrong move. Worst of all, it erodes the trust between you.

Wolfdogs are often more sensitive than doggie-dogs. *While all dogs should be trained with positive methods, it is especially crucial with wolfdogs.* The use of harsh training methods could result in severe psychological damage to your wolfdog, not to mention severe injury to you, either immediately or down the road. Now for the good news: There are wonderful, effective, positive ways to train your wolfdog!

It's nice to believe that your wolfdog wants to please you, and for all I know, maybe he does. But the truth is, *canines do what works for them.* Well, that's understandable. So do humans! Let's use that knowledge to our advantage. The fact that your wolfdog will work for a reward, whether that means treats, praise, petting or something else, makes reward-based, positive training easy and effective. Turn the page for some basic principles to get you started...

1. **Canines learn by association.** When training a new behavior, it is very important that the reward closely follow the desired behavior. For example, when teaching your wolfdog to walk next to you on leash, the praise and treat should be given as he is in position next to you, not after he's begun to lag behind. On the other side of the coin, reprimanding your wolfdog for something he may have done hours ago (i.e. you come home to find your running shoes shredded) is pointless; he won't associate your yelling with what he's done. If it happens often enough, he may well begin to fear your arrival home, as you're always angry for no reason he can fathom.

2. **Reward the behaviors you want, rather than punishing those you don't want.** Most of us are so conditioned to look for things our wolfdogs are doing wrong, that it takes an adjustment on our part to begin noticing and rewarding those things they're doing right. For example, when your wolfdog whines because he wants attention, you might yell at him to be quiet. But what about when he's lying calmly? Most of us never think about rewarding calm behavior. The result is a wolfdog who gets rewarded with our attention (even yelling is attention to him) when he whines or barks, but is ignored when he lies quietly. Think about what we're teaching him! If, on the other hand, he gets attention for being calm, he will be calm more often...which brings us to #3...

3. **That which is rewarded is more likely to happen again.** This is a very powerful principle, and is the foundation of reward-based training. Consider the wolfdog who virtually flies to his owner upon hearing the word, "Cookie!" Why does he do it? Because that lucky dog has been given a cookie every time he's ever heard that word. Smart owners build a history of positive reinforcement by rewarding their dogs each time they come when called, so they are likely to respond correctly the next time. On

the flip side, it is all too easy to unwittingly reward behaviors we *don't* want, thereby causing them to happen again. For example, when a pup jumps up on us, many of us reach down to pet the adorable furball. The jumping up will more than likely continue, as the pup has been rewarded for it by our petting him.

4. Punishment is anything that causes the behavior to occur less frequently. I hesitate to even include punishment in this book, since I do not advocate it in any way; but it is important to understand the concept. For punishment to be effective, it has to make such an impression that the animal discontinues the behavior. If you are continually jerking an animal with a choke chain as you walk along, you are punishing him ineffectively, over and over. (Besides, he will eventually habituate to the pressure, thereby necessitating even harsher corrections.) In other words, if the behavior continues, the punishment was not effective. Unfortunately, people usually react to obviously ineffective punishment with harsher punishment. Heck, if it didn't work the first time, we'll just do it harder! Not only are continued attempts to punish ineffective, the whole approach is cruel. *If it didn't work the first time, it's not going to.* I suggest that if you are already using punishment methods and are finding that they don't stop the unwanted behavior, *stop using them!* It's not helping, and may well be harming your relationship, not to mention your wolfdog's physical and psychological well-being. You wouldn't continue to take a medication that wasn't working; it doesn't make sense to continue an ineffective course of treatment with your wolfdog, either. Consider using positive methods instead. You have nothing to lose and everything to gain. I can assure you that if properly implemented, your wolfdog will respond better and your bond will be all the stronger for it.

5. **Extinction** *If a behavior is ignored, it will eventually extinguish on its own*, like an unattended cigarette. Imagine that you want to buy a soda from a vending machine. You drop your change in, press the button and wait. Nothing happens. You start pressing the button more forcefully, and try a few others as well. You jangle the change lever. No soda, no change. If you're like me, you might at that point shake or kick the machine. (I never said I was patient.) Can you believe it, all this and still no soda! Grumbling to yourself, you give up and leave. In this example, the behavior extinguished because there was no payoff, no reward. Me kicking or shaking the machine is an example of an *extinction burst* (not to be confused with a cranky redhead). This means that before your wolfdog stops the behavior entirely, it may actually get worse. The important thing is to be aware of this so that you can ride it out when it happens. Just remember that the extinction burst is actually a good thing, as it predicts the end of the behavior.

Here is a real-life example where extinction would be useful: Since my two fur-kids don't sleep in the bedroom, they scratch at the door each morning to let us know they've decided it's time for breakfast. (And no, this scenario is not high on my list of ways to establish great leadership.) If we were to simply ignore the scratching, what would likely happen is that it would continue for a while. Eventually there would be an extinction burst; the scratching would get more intense. After that, it would most likely stop altogether. Why? Because they're not getting rewarded for their efforts with any attention whatsoever. The hard part is waiting out situations like this, especially at six a.m. when it's easier to just give in, feed them and go back to bed. Obviously we haven't solved this one at our home, as my husband does get out of bed to feed them when they demand it. Have I mentioned that training the two-leggeds is the hard part?!

6. Positive reinforcement is something the animal wants. Just because you think those new, expensive treats are a great reward doesn't mean your fur-kid agrees. If he turns his nose up at them, they're not going to be of much use in training. One of Mojo's favorite things in the world is banana. Go figure. It's not a traditional training treat, but if that's what floats his boat, you bet I'm going to use it! A reward can be petting, verbal praise, a throw of the ball, a quick game of tug, sniffing grass, saying hello to another dog, etc. The sky's the limit—and if you're a good trainer, you'll consider all the things your wolfdog finds rewarding, and use them in your training.

7. Jackpot! When I was a kid, my Norwegian cousin would send me a spoon every Christmas. (No, this isn't some crazy Norwegian tradition.) Each spoon was a precious little enameled masterpiece, part of a serving set. Unfortunately, I was ten years old at the time and had no interest in formal dinners, unless macaroni and cheese was somehow involved. Whenever one of these packages would arrive, I'd carefully unwrap it, admire the spoon, then hand it over to my mother for safekeeping. As you might guess, the arrival of these packages did not cause me to turn cartwheels. Then one Christmas, something magical happened. I opened the package to find...a necklace! A beautiful, shiny, silver heart! Jackpot! While the spoons were nice enough, you can bet that silver necklace really got my attention.

A jackpot is something really special, head and shoulders above the usual reward. Your wolfdog can earn this amazing prize by doing something especially wonderful. While it is important to use treats that your wolfdog likes during training, save the Super-Yummy, Best-Thing-In-The-World treat as a jackpot. For Mojo, that would be his beloved bananas. Here's an example of how I'd use the jackpot: In teaching Sit, I realize that while Mojo obviously understands the behavior, he doesn't sit very quickly. Each time I give the cue, he watches me for a moment, then languidly lowers his butt to the floor. You can almost hear him thinking, *Oh, okay, if I must.* He earns a low-value treat, perhaps a piece of kibble. However, on the fourth repetition, he responds immediately. Butt hits floor in record time. Jackpot! I immediately give him a piece of banana, along with effusive praise and petting. This makes an impression on Mojo, calling his attention to the fact that he's done something really wonderful. He is more likely to perform this behavior better than usual the next time. A jackpot doesn't have to be food, either. If your wolfdog is like my German Shepherd and lives for a toss of the ball, use that as your jackpot. Know your wolfdog and use what works for him.

8. **Counter-Conditioning** Nope, that doesn't mean conditioning your wolfdog to stay off counters. What it does mean is that when you want your wolfdog to stop doing something, you *give him something else to do instead—an incompatible behavior.* In other words, you "condition" a behavior which is "counter" to the undesirable one. A woman I ran into at the post office recently could have benefited from this concept. She had a small boy with her. The child was just tall enough to reach the counter, and kept knocking things off it as she tried to talk to the clerk. Each time the child knocked something down, she'd hiss at him to stop. The boy would stop, then start up again when she looked away. Mom got increasingly frustrated. Her transaction finally complete, she grabbed the boy by the hand and left in a huff. Had she given the child something else to do (*"Honey, it would help Mommy sooo much if you could hold this small package for me, that's it, hold it with both hands, thank you, what a good boy!"*), the child wouldn't have been physically able to do so and knock things off the counter at the same time. Hmm I guess that one really *is* an example of *counter* conditioning!

The same principle applies to your wolfdog. Is he jumping up on you? Have him sit instead. He can't sit and jump at the same time. Chewing on furniture? Give him a legal chewie; he can't chew on both at once. (Okay, he probably *can*, but most won't.) On a blank piece of paper, draw a line down the middle. On the left side, list all the things your wolfdog does that you'd like him to stop. On the right, next to each one, write down an incompatible behavior that he could do instead. Once you start thinking about things in this way, you'll be surprised at the creative solutions you come up with—and how unnecessary punishment really is.

9. **Be consistent.** Consistency is one of the cornerstones of successful training. The more consistent you are, the faster your wolfdog will grasp what is expected of him. Use the same word and tone of voice for the same behavior. For example, "down" should always mean lie down, and not be used sometimes for "Off the furniture." Everyone should be on the same page about which verbal cue means what. Consistency also means that all family members and friends understand and abide by the ground rules. For example, no wolfdogs on the couch means no wolfdogs on the couch, *ever*. Behaviors can't be okay for the wolfdog to do with one person and not with another. A specific behavior should earn the same response, regardless of who he engages.

A fun and useful project for kids is to make a Human-to-Woof Dictionary. Depending on your kids' age, on each page, either you or they write the verbal cue first, then the behavior it refers to. The kids can then draw pictures underneath. For example, a typical page might have DOWN written across the top, with "Timber Lies Down" under that. The rest of the page would have a drawing of Timber lying there with a big toothy grin!

A wonderful thing about reward-based training is that even when we humans are inconsistent, the animal is not harmed (as he might be with inconsistent or badly timed punishment). Besides, once a behavior is learned, going to random reinforcement (inconsistent rewards) only strengthens the behavior!

10. **Raise criteria gradually.** Raise criteria (what your wolfdog is being asked to do) in small increments, building on each success. For example, when teaching your wolfdog to stay, start with a very short stay, i.e. three seconds. When that is successful, ask for a stay which is, say, two seconds longer. If the five-second stay is too much (your wolfdog gets up), don't correct him. You've asked for too much too soon. Simply go back to three seconds and start again. Raising criteria gradually eliminates the need for correction by setting your wolfdog up to succeed.

Wolf Park wolves are taught, with food rewards, to push a spool

Food rewards motivate your wolfdog and communicate to him that he's performed a behavior correctly. Once the behavior has been learned, begin to vary reinforcement in two ways: One, vary the actual reward. Begin to throw in praise, petting, a quick toss of the ball or a game with a favorite toy in lieu of food. In ten repetitions, make eight food treats and two alternate rewards. Then take that number down to six food treats and four alternates, etc. This keeps things interesting and begins to wean your wolfdog off food treats. Two, vary the rate of reinforcement. Don't reward for every repetition of a behavior your wolfdog already knows. If you're working on sit, begin to reward only the fastest or straightest sits. Be careful not to make your schedule of reinforcement predictable. In other words, don't reward, for example, every third sit. If you do, your wolfdog, smart little bugger that he is, will figure out quickly that he doesn't have to put much effort into repetitions one and two. Using these methods, your wolfdog will learn to respond even when you don't have treats obviously on your person. *Note*: Don't make treats obvious. If he performs the behavior correctly, run with your fur-kid to get a treat, all the while praising like crazy! Your wolfdog should think you're a magician who can pull treats out of thin air.

Most of all, remember that training should be fun! Don't train when you're grouchy. Keep sessions short and lively, and always end on a successful note. If your wolfdog has serious behavioral issues, contact an experienced trainer who uses positive methods. Obedience training can be learned in a group setting (which provides excellent socialization as well) or in your own home. To find a good trainer in your area, contact the Association of Pet Dog Trainers (APDT), an organization dedicated to the ongoing education of their members and the promotion of positive training methods. (See *Resources*.)

Questions and Answers

These questions have been taken from actual e-mails, phone calls and other requests for advice over the years. Some names have been changed, letters edited, and some are composites of questions received.

Q: *My wolfdog is four months old. We haven't had any major problems with her other than the usual puppy stuff, but one thing she does drives us crazy! She loves to grab things and run away with them. She's made off with my kids' socks, artificial flowers, you name it. We chase her but by the time we get the stuff back we're worn out and the stuff is destroyed. What can we do to stop her? Will she outgrow this?*

A: What you're describing is a great game for canines, called "Keep-Away." You grab something, make sure the silly human sees you, and the chase is on! Whee! The way to stop this game is two-fold. One involves management. That means your kids' socks, along with anything else you don't want grabbed, are kept out of your wolfdog's reach. Second, don't play the game. When your wolfdog grabs something and runs with it, sit down and look bored. Don't even watch him. Chances are, he'll dart in closer and closer to you, wondering, *What's wrong with this human? Why won't she chase me?* If you ignore him long enough, he may even put the object in your hand, or close enough. When he does, take it and say "Thank you." Give him a treat and a petting. (Of course, if the object he's absconded with is valuable to you or dangerous to him, by all means, get it away from him immediately.) Try the ignoring tactic first, but if he runs off into another room where he's likely tearing the thing apart or ingesting it, grab a piece of hot dog from the kitchen, go to him and trade

163

for the forbidden object. Trading shouldn't become a habit, but will do in an emergency. In the meantime, work on a reliable recall (see *"I Just Want Him to Come..."*) and a solid "Leave It" (see *"Off"*). Once he's got those down, the next time he runs off with something call him to you, ask him to leave the object, then make a great, happy fuss and either play a game with him or give him something even better in return. (Just make sure *he* thinks it's something better, too.)

Q: *What's your opinion of the invisible fencing type containment? Is it effective?*

A: I don't think much of this type of containment for wolfdogs. For one thing, it involves the use of a "shock collar." Each time your wolfdog touches the invisible barrier, a shock is delivered to his neck. These devices are not appropriate for wolfdogs (nor, in my opinion, are they appropriate for *any* living being). Wolfdogs can be extremely sensitive and being shocked around the neck could cause psychological damage and produce even more "skittishness." Besides, it's cruel! Another reason this type of containment is not a good idea, is that if the wolfdog crosses the barrier and gets shocked going through, he's not very likely to come back in. Plus, this type of fence does not present much of a visual barrier. Consider whether you'd want small children coming up to it, trying to visit your wolfdog. A solid, visible form of containment such as chain link is preferable. For containment issues, please refer to my first book, *Living with Wolfdogs*.

Q. *My Husky/wolf loves to roll around on her back in the foulest-smelling stuff she can find. She even rolled in the guts of a dead animal when we went hiking. Why do they do this? It's disgusting!*

A. What? You don't enjoy the very finest of doggie perfumes?! Okay, you're right, it's not one of our fur-kids' most endearing habits. The behavior you describe is called *scent-rolling*. Wolves do it, wolfdogs do it, and some doggie-dogs do it, though biologists have never agreed upon why. One explanation is that wolves roll on dead animals to bring the scent back to the rest of the pack, so they know the carcass is out there. Whatever the reason, being an instinctive behavior, scent-rolling would be tough to eliminate through training. Your best bet is to keep her on leash around potential scent-rolling items. Or, you could use the ever-helpful "Leave It" as she approaches the mess, before she's had a chance to roll in it.

Q: *I have two high content wolfdogs who live in an outdoor pen. They get lots of attention. In fact, they're spoiled rotten! The only real problem is that they howl. They used to howl once or twice during the day, but now it's at all hours of the night, for long, non-stop sessions. This may be because there have been more sirens in our neighborhood lately. Though I don't live in a busy city, there are houses nearby and I'm worried that my neighbors will complain. Is there anything I can do to stop this?*

A: I can sympathize. Howling is a beautiful, magical sound—but not at 4:00 a.m.! There is a product I would recommend you try, called the Kennel Silencer (see *Resources*). This ultrasonic device is basically a small black box that hangs outside your pen and plugs into a nearby electrical outlet. When woofers howl, a sound is triggered which only they can hear (though you can set it to human-audible if you wish). You'll know it's gone off, because most likely the howl will be cut short after a second or so, and your wolfdogs will probably dart across the pen away from the box. A built-in dial allows you to control the level of sensitivity. The sensor works up to roughly 25 feet from the sound source. Most canines learn quickly that when the box is plugged in, they need to keep quiet. You could plug it in before going to sleep (let them see you do this), then make a show of unplugging it in the morning, saying "Okay!" so they know they're free to make noise if they want to. Technically, this device is a bit on the aversive side, and I prefer to use positive methods whenever possible. But when you measure it against the possibility of losing your animals or harm coming to them, it doesn't seem all that bad.

Note: Please do not confuse the Kennel Silencer with the type of silencer which entails your wolfdog wearing a collar which would shock him when he makes noise. I do not recommend shock collars!

Q: *My wife and I have done our research, found a breeder we like, and are planning to get a wolf hybrid pup. My question is, this breeder is trying to sell us two pups at once. Should we get one or both? How important is it that our pup have a playmate at this age? The pups would be six weeks old when we take them home.*

A: I would recommend that you get one pup at a time. Yes, wolfdogs are pack animals and they should have a companion. But at such a young age, there are a few good reasons to have one pup alone first. At six weeks, your pup is going through a crucial bonding period. He's just been taken from his littermates and his mother, and will naturally bond with you and your family. If there is another pup around, he will most likely bond closely with the other pup, and may not bond as closely with you. That's why some owners, when getting two pups, limit the pups' interactions with each other. They spend time with the pups separately and then supervise short puppy play sessions. If you decide to get both pups at once, I would recommend you do the same.

Another reason to get one pup first is training and housebreaking. For housebreaking to be successful, you must be hyper-vigilant. You will need to keep an eye on that pup constantly. This is much easier when you have one to watch than two. As far as training is concerned, it is very difficult to train two pups at once. Why not get one housebroken and trained first, then get the second?

I am not suggesting that you keep your pup isolated by any means. Young pups do require socialization with other canines and people (see *Socialization*). Even if you do get both pups, don't assume that covers their socialization needs. They should still meet other canines. Also, be sure to separate them for brief periods. If you don't, you may end up with best buddies who, as they mature, scream and panic when they are separated. Case in point: In one of my dog training classes, an older gentleman brought his two Huskies. They were seven and ten years old, bless his heart (and no, they were not too old to learn a thing or two!). He'd had them together since puppyhood, and they'd never been separated, even briefly. When we did exercises that required one to be walked a few feet away from the other, they would make the most unholy screaming sounds you've ever heard. Trust me, you want to avoid that type of scenario if you can.

Lastly, you didn't say whether these pups are from the same litter (I assume they are), or what sex they are. There is a lot of anecdotal evidence about littermates fighting with each other as they mature. As far as gender, I would strongly advise against getting two same-sex pups. Same-sex wolfdogs are much more likely to fight as they mature, especially females.

Q: *I hope you can settle a bet between me and my girlfriend. She doesn't believe me that my dog actually has any wolf in him. I told her she doesn't know what she's talking about. He obviously does! He's got the webbing between his toes and that dark spot on his tail. Doesn't that prove it?*

A: Hope you've got a slice of humble pie in the fridge—your girlfriend wins the bet. Webbing between the toes is not a sure sign of being a wolfdog, any more than it's a sure sign of being a duck. Many dogs have toe-webbing, especially those bred to work in water. As for the pre-caudal, or "scent gland" (that dark spot on his tail), it's found in many dogs and is easy to spot on many northern breeds. Don't feel badly; there is a lot of misinformation out there about "sure signs" of a dog having wolf in them. Most of these are characteristics that dogs share, and some are downright weird. In addition to the scent gland and webbing criteria, here are a few I've heard over the years. They all start out with "I know he's a wolf because..."

"He's got those ice blue eyes;"
"His tail hangs straight down;"
"She has those retractable claws, like a cat;"
"His eyes are red when I photograph him at night;"
"She sucks water instead of lapping it;"
"He's got those extra teeth at the back;"
...and the ever-popular, "The breeder told me so."

Huskies have blue eyes. Wolves don't, except as pups until about eight weeks of age (and even then they're a dark blue). Many dogs have tails which hang straight down. Wolves don't have retractable claws. Photography can make anyone's eyes look red...or iridescent green, for that matter. (Does that make them an alien?) The sucking vs. lapping... I don't know what to say. That one's always baffled me, and I've heard it more than once. Wolves and dogs have the same amount of teeth—forty-two. As far as the breeder telling you so, use common sense. They are by definition trying to sell you an animal. Not all breeders are unscrupulous, but some will say anything to make a buck.

While there are no sure signs that your wolfdog has wolf in him, there *are* a few signs that will tell you that your animal is *not* a pure wolf. One of those is having a pink nose. A pure wolf's nose is black. A wolfdog's nose, however, may be pink. Another qualifying factor is what time of year the animal was born. Female wolves give birth once a year, after a 63 day gestation period, during the spring months. Nature set it up that way so the pups have an optimum chance of survival. Although there can be some individual variation, male wolves are only fertile from December

Note the dark spot on tail, the pre-caudal or "scent gland"

through March. (Though male wolves have been known to produce sperm as early as late October and as late as early May, the counts in October/November and April/May were so low that is is unlikely that these males could have fathered pups during these periods - Sloan, Wolf Park.) Arctic wolves, however, can be born through the first week of June. So if you have "papers" claiming your wolfdog has a pure wolf parent, but the pup was born in October, for example, you can be sure that something is awry. If both parents are wolfdogs, this hard and fast rule does not apply, but keep in mind that the higher the wolf content, the more the animal should cycle like a pure wolf.

Q. *I feed my wolfdog dry dog food. He is doing fine on it, but the problem is, he just about inhales it! Is there anything I can do to slow his eating down? I worry about medical problems.*

A. There are a few things you can try. One is to feed his meal in a Kong® (see *Kongs and Other Sanity-Preservers*). Another is to place a large stone or brick in the bottom of his dish, then pour the kibble over it. He will then have to eat carefully around the object. Or, taking this idea a step further, take a heavy metal chain and coil it in the bottom of the food dish, so it forms a spiral. Pour the kibble over it. Your woofer will have to be even more careful than with the brick, to get the pieces out from around and inside the links. That ought to slow him down!

Q. *We recently adopted a Husky/wolf mix pup from a rescue center. While she is fine with me, she has a habit of urinating a teeny bit whenever my husband comes home. Is this normal?*

A. What you're describing is *submissive urination*, which is not uncommon in puppies. Your pup is most likely intimidated by your husband, and this is her way of showing it. (Pups may urinate when excited as well.) The worst thing anyone could do when she does this is to reprimand her. Doing so would only scare her and make the problem worse. If possible, greet her outside so that your carpeting is not ruined. When your husband comes home, have him gently (with small motions) toss a treat on the floor near her without looking at her. It may help to shift her perception of him from fear to *Mmm, goodies*. If even the food tossing is too much for her, have your husband ignore her completely when he first walks in. When he does greet her, he should use calming signals (see *Understanding Canine Body Language and Signals*) to put her at ease and let her know he's not a threat. The good news about submissive urination is, most pups grow out of it.

Resources

Recommended Books/Videos

Most of these books and videos are available through Dogwise (formerly Direct Book Service) at 1-800-776-2665 or www.dogwise.com.

Training & Behavior

Dog Language: An Encyclopedia of Canine Behavior
Roger Abrantes (Denmark)
Denmark: Wakan Tanka, Inc., 1997 ISBN 0-96604-840-7

Dog-Friendly Dog Training
Andrea Arden
New York, NY: Howell Books, 1999 ISBN 1-582450099

The Culture Clash
Jean Donaldson
Oakland, CA: James & Kenneth Publishers, 1996 ISBN 1-888047-05-4

Dogs Are From Neptune
Jean Donaldson
Montreal, Quebec: Lasar Multimedia Productions Inc., 1998
ISBN 0-9684207-1-0

How to Teach a New Dog Old Tricks
Ian Dunbar
Oakland, CA: James & Kenneth Publishers, 1991 ISBN 1-888047-03-8

Sirius Puppy Training (video)
Ian Dunbar
Oakland, CA: James & Kenneth, 1987

Wolfdogs A-Z

Dog Behavior: An Owner's Guide to a Happy Healthy Pet
Ian Dunbar
IDG Books Worldwide, 1998 ISBN: 0876052367

Books by Dr. Dunbar may be purchased through most Barnes & Nobles and
Borders Book Stores, or ordered directly from the publisher at James & Kenneth
Publishers, 2140 Shattuck Avenue #2406, Berkeley, CA 94704
(510) 658-8588.

The Cautious Canine
Patricia B. McConnell, Ph.D.
Black Earth, WI: Dog's Best Friend, Ltd., 1998 ISBN 1-891767-00-3

Don't Shoot the Dog
Karen Pryor
New York: Bantam Books, Inc., 1984 ISBN 0-553-25388-3

The Toolbox for Remodeling Your Problem Dog
Terry Ryan
New York, NY: Simon & Schuster, 1998 ISBN 0-87605-049-6

Clicker Training

Take A Bow Wow I & II (videos on trick training)
Virginia Broitman & Sherry Lipman

Click and Go (video)
Dr. Deb Jones

Clicker Training For Dogs
Karen Pryor
Sunshine Books, Inc., 1999 ISBN 1-89094-800-4

Karen Pryor's Clicker Training Start-Up Kit
Karen Pryor

Click and Treat Training Kit (video/booklet/clicker)
Gary Wilkes

Clickers, Target Sticks, Bait Bags & More

www.dogwise.com
www.legacy-by-mail.com
www.sitstay.com

Other Publications

The Whole Dog Journal
(Monthly publication, focuses on natural dog care/training)
Subscriptions 1-800-829-9165
Back issues 1-800-424-7887

Health and Nutrition

Give Your Dog A Bone
Dr. Ian Billinghurst
N.S.W. Australia: Ian Billinghurst, 1993 ISBN 0-646-16028-1

The Natural Dog: A Complete Guide For Caring Owners
Mary L. Brennan, D.V.M.
New York, NY: Penguin Books, 1993 ISBN 0-452-27019-7

The Healing Touch : The Proven Massage Program for
Cats and Dogs
Michael W. Fox
New York: Newmarket Press, 1990 ISBN 1-55704-062-1

Bach Flower Remedies for Animals
Helen Graham & Gregory Vlamis
Scotland: Findhorn Press, 1999 ISBN 1-899171-72-X

*Dr. Pitcairn's Complete Guide to Natural Health
for Dogs & Cats*
Pitcairn and Pitcairn
Emmaus, PA: Rodale Press, 1995 ISBN 0-87596-243-2

Natural Nutrition for Dogs and Cats
Kymythy R. Schultze
Carlsbad, CA: Hay House, 1998 ISBN 1-56170-636-1

Natural Healing for Dogs & Cats
Diane Stein
Freedom, CA: The Crossing Press, Inc., 1993 ISBN 0-89594-686-6

*The Tellington TTouch : A Revolutionary Natural Method
to Train and Care for Your Favorite Animal*
Linda Tellington-Jones
New York, NY: Penguin, 1995 ISBN: 0-14011-728-8

The Holistic Guide for a Healthy Dog
W. Volhard & D. Brown, DVM
New York, NY: Macmillan, 1995 ISBN 0-87605-560-9

Miscellaneous Books

Agility Tricks for Improved Attention, Flexibility & Confidence
Donna Duford
Clean Run Productions, 1999

Fun Nosework For Dogs
Roy Hunter
United Kingdom: Howlin' Moon Press, 1996 ISBN 1-88899-403-7

Fun and Games with Dogs
Roy Hunter
United Kingdom: Howlin' Moon Press, 1995 ISBN 1-88899-400-2

Simply Scenting® (scent discrimination)
Dawn Jecs
Puyallup, WA: Choose To Heel®,1995

On Talking Terms with Dogs: Calming Signals
Turid Rugaas
Kula, HI: Legacy, 1997

Other Book Sources

Amazon
www.amazon.com

Wolf Dunn website
www.inetdesign.com/wolfdunn
Note: The Wolf Dunn operates the Wolfdog Mailing List.
Proceeds from ordering through this web site help to keep
the list up and running.

Wolfshadow Books (hard to find/out of print
wolf-related books)
200 Route 46
Mine Hill, New Jersey 07803
(973) 366-5780

Wolfdogs A-Z

Miscellaneous

Kennel Silencer
Texmark
1-800-451-0615

Association of Pet Dog Trainers (APDT)
66 Morris Avenue #2A
Springfield, N.J. 07081
1-800-PET-DOGS
www.apdt.com (contains searchable database of trainers)

National Wolfdog Alliance, Inc.
P.O. Box 2757
Loves Park, IL 61132-2757
http://www.wolfdogalliance.org
A coalition of wolf-dog organizations and enthusiasts
dedicated to responsible wolfdog ownership.
Educational information, help and guidance.

Socialization

Early socialization is one of the best gifts you can give your wolfdog. If your fur-kid is a pup, you have an amazing opportunity. By exposing him to various people, animals, objects, sounds and locations, you can help him develop into a confident canine who is comfortable in most situations. Many experiences which are potentially traumatizing to a wolfdog can be rendered less frightening by safe, early exposure to those things.

Don't Put Off Tomorrow...

The critical socialization period for canines is roughly between three and twelve weeks of age. During this time, new people and situations are most easily accepted. Once the juvenile period starts, at approximately twelve weeks of age, there is a growing tendency to react fearfully to novel stimuli. For this reason, exposure to new things should be initiated before twelve weeks of age. The socialization period for wolfdogs is the same as for doggie-dogs. Don't assume, though, that supplying plenty of socialization during this critical period alone is sufficient to set your pup up for life! Continuing social interaction is necessary so that your pup does not "backslide" and become desocialized.

Traditional wisdom cautioned canine owners not to let their dogs interact with other dogs until they had undergone a full series of inoculations, culminating in the rabies vaccination at four months of age. Modern trainers understand the importance of having your dog socialize with other canines before that. Naturally, you don't want to take your pup to a park where other dogs have been, as it is possible for him to contract a disease from a sick dog who has been there, even if that dog is no longer present. Does a friend or neighbor have a healthy, well-socialized dog who yours could play with? It is essential that your pup learn proper canine interactions, based on body language and signals. Well-adjusted adult dogs are excellent teachers. Wolfdogs who have been removed from their litter too early may not have learned to play properly, or not to bite down too hard (*bite inhibition*).

A wolfdog who has not been properly socialized may be fearful of other canines. A puppy play group can help. These groups are becoming increasingly popular. Look for one that accepts pups under four months of age. A good puppy group provides safe, supervised play sessions and may also address problem behaviors and/or offer introductory obedience training. Ask your vet or local training center for a referral.

It's Never Too Late

Though early learning of social skills and exposure to novel stimuli is preferred, all is not lost for the wolfdog who has not had those advantages. To the contrary, many wolfdogs who have been rehomed as adults have made great progress in accepting new people, dogs and situations.

Even wolfdogs who are territorial can have a social life. If yours is possessive of your own back yard, arrange a play session at a friend's house; if both canines are territorial, meet at a local park. When introducing your wolfdog to other dogs, it's fine to have him on-leash, but *don't keep the leash tight*. Canines can get defensive when restrained. Keep the leash slack, breathe, and monitor the situation. Try not to position the dogs nose to nose, dead-on. Instead, approach with loose leash, from a slight angle—it's much less confrontational from the canine point of view.

Have A Little Class

A wonderful way to expose your wolfdog to other canines is to join a group obedience class. Group classes, which traditionally accepted dogs from six months of age on, now begin much younger and can prevent a variety of behavior problems. A group class affords the opportunity for your companion to be around other dogs in a controlled environment. Be sure to find out what methods your instructor uses. *I can not emphasize enough that you should seek out an instructor who uses positive methods.* Don't just call and say "Do you use positive methods?" You're not likely to find someone who answers, "Nope. I jest drop-kick them li'l suckers 'cross the floor iffin' they don' lissen!" Ask instead whether they use treats in their training (this is good); ask if they use choke chains (this is not desirable); ask what their general training philosophy is. Don't feel shy about asking questions! A good, professional instructor will be happy to respond, and should be agreeable to you observing one of their classes.

The impact training can have on your wolfdog, positive or negative, is immeasurable. For help on finding a competent, positive trainer in your area, contact the APDT or visit their web site (see *Resources*). If you find yourself in a class where you're uncomfortable with the methods being used, let your instructor know. If no alternatives can be found, leave. *Do not assume that the instructor knows more than you do about what's good for your wolfdog.* They may have lots of experience, but not every method is suitable for every canine. Follow your instincts!

Many trainers are hesitant about having wolfdogs in their classes. If your wolfdog is so low content that he looks and acts pretty much like a dog, you might want to just call him, for example, a Husky mix. If your wolfdog does, however, look and/or act wolfy, ask the instructor whether they will accept a wolfdog in class. If they seem hesitant, see if they'll meet with you to assess yours as an individual. You might have a chance to do some education, as many trainers have not worked with wolfdogs before and may initially balk at the idea. So change their minds. Personally, I'm thrilled when a wolfdog signs up for one of my classes. The hard part is not playing favorites!

Who Are You?

It is important to socialize your wolfdog to people of all types. This includes children, men, women, people of various skin colors, large adults, short adults, those with facial hair, elderly people and those in uniforms, to name a few. Children in particular can trigger a fear reaction if your wolfdog has not been socialized with them. Children move and vocalize differently than adults, and can seem unpredictable and frightening to canines. My husband and I do not have kids, nor do we plan to; we prefer the four-footed kind. As most of our friends don't have kids either, Mojo was not exposed to many children as a pup. Sure, there were kids at the park, but he had little interaction with them. It was my mistake not to seek out children for him to interact with in a positive way when he was young. Like so many canines who are not exposed to children early on, he is now frightened of them. Unfortunately, his fear looks a lot like aggression. Mojo's reaction is to raise his hackles, lower his head, and growl threateningly. Obviously, I do not bring children and Mojo together in any way. But I *should* be able to, and so should you with your own wolfdog. This is especially important if you plan to have children. (Note: It *is* possible, over time, to desensitize canines like Mojo with children. We have chosen to carefully manage the situation instead.)

If you have friends with children who are relatively calm, invite them over and introduce them to your wolfdog. Teach the kids to approach calmly and quietly, and not to hover over him. Have them make a fist with palm facing down, place their hand under his nose, and let him sniff. They should never come down over his head with an open palm, as kids tend to do. I usually demonstrate by coming at the kids both ways; that palm coming down overhead looks scary, and it usually gets the point across. Let kids know what the rules are for proper interaction—no sudden movements, no yelling, slapping, pulling, etc. As for your wolfdog, having kids around is a good time to enforce the "no jumping" rule (see *Jumping Up...*). If your wolfdog gets too mouthy, have the children hold a toy or ball between them and him. If you notice your wolfdog getting stressed, or his excitement escalating too much, end the visit or take a break. Try to discern what caused his reaction, and adjust that factor at the next session.

Many wolfdogs are skittish around new people, especially when those people are male. If yours is this way, ask people to let your wolfdog approach in his own good time. *Never* force your wolfdog to be near or have someone pet him if he is not comfortable with it. I knew a guy who did this with his pure wolves on a regular basis. His method of getting a wolf to overcome shyness with people was to drag the poor thing, cowering and cringing, over to the person, who would then pet him. His animals all grew, without exception, into skittish, miserable animals who ended up in rescues or euthanized. Instead, have people use calming signals (see *Understanding Body Language and Signals*) such as turning away, yawning and lip-licking. This will help to put your wolfdog at ease. Be sure too that people don't hover *over* your wolfdog. I was in an enclosure with a pure wolf once who seemed as though he was enjoying the attentions of the four people surrounding him. When one woman innocently leaned over to kiss him on top of the head, he snapped at her. Be careful, and let others know how to behave as well.

C'mon, C'mon now Touch Me...

Another important thing for your wolfdog to get accustomed to is being handled. Gradually desensitize him to the types of motions kids might make, such as grabbing at his fur or tugging at his ears, by doing them gently yourself. Keep the mood light and even silly. Teach him to be calm too as children run and play, by reinforcing with treats and petting as he sits or lays quietly in their presence.

Getting your wolfdog accustomed to handling now will make future vet visits and grooming sessions much less stressful for both him and the professionals involved. Do daily massage sessions, paying particular attention to getting your fur-kid comfortable with having his ears, mouth and paws handled.

At Wolf Park, a wolf education and research facility in Battleground, Indiana, the "Bunny Lesson" is initiated with all captive wolves at an early age. The technique is used to desensitize the wolves there to being manipulated during medical procedures, and is a good example of how early handling can make all the difference in a canine's acceptance of it as an adult. Jill Porter explains:

"We have the wolf sit with its back to us, facing forward. We then gently scratch its chest as we lean it back toward our knees.

We continue scratching along the chest and belly, wherever the animal seems to enjoy it most. If done right, it will trigger the scratch reflex and get the back feet kicking—hence the name 'bunny lesson.' As this is done, someone can hold off a vein in the foreleg and draw blood, or do any other medical procedure desired. We may vary this technique by letting the animal chew on a hard toy, or hand treats to it, or even cover its face with a hat if that doesn't stress or scare the animal or cause them to try to eat the hat. The idea is to keep the animal relaxed and enjoying the procedure and not feel restrained. If at any time the animal struggles to get up, we let them up and try again later. Since wolves have little or no tolerance for restraint, we find that this method of 'voluntary' restraint works well. The idea is to make the animal

want to stay, not to force it to stay. We have used this method quite successfully for many years in a variety of medical procedures. We also find it beneficial to practice this from the time the animal is young, and practice often after that. We have taught it to adult wolves as well. The key is to always make it pleasant and end on a good note."

Training Sit, Down and Stay

Sit, Down and Stay are basic behaviors that are very helpful for your wolfdog to know. The good news is, they are simple to teach and easy for your wolfdog to learn.

Sit Happens

Stand with your wolfdog facing you. Hold a food treat just above his nose, then move it slowly back over the top of his muzzle, continuing over his head. (Do not raise the treat too high or your wolfdog will jump up for it.) If you do this correctly, your wolfdog should track the treat with his nose and eyes, tilting his head backward until his butt touches the floor. If you are using a clicker, click as his rear hits the floor. Whether clicking or not, give the treat while he's still in sitting position, along with a "Good boy!"

If you happen to have one of those wolfdogs who keeps backing up but won't sit when you lure him in this way, try backing him into a corner. Once his rear is against the wall and his head moves up and back to track the food, he has little choice but to sit. Alternately, if you are working with another person but there are no walls handy, have the other person keep their legs close together with toes pointed outward to form a corner. (A good friend should not only help you train, but perform ballet on demand!) Maneuver your wolfdog backward into the V created by their legs. As soon as you feel your wolfdog definitely understands the behavior, begin to fade the lure by making the motion with your hand, without the treat in it. Reward from the other hand.

Some wolfdogs are fearful of anything overhead, including your hands. If this is the case, do not use the lure-reward method.

187

Luring over the head and rewarding when Sit happens!

Instead, wait until your wolfdog happens to sit, then either click or say "Yes!" and treat. This is called "capturing" the behavior. To increase your odds of getting Sit to happen, go to a boring room in your house, then wait. Or, turn on your television and ignore your wolfdog. He will more than likely sit. If you're too impatient to wait for offered sits, you can always use the modeling method (though I prefer non-hands-on whenever possible): Place one hand on your wolfdog's chest and the other on his rump. Push gently into his chest and down on his rump at the same time. This will effectively place him in a sit position. Even though he hasn't done the sit voluntarily, reward as though he had. If your wolfdog resists or becomes uncomfortable when you attempt this method, don't push it. Try the capturing method instead.

Do lots of practice repetitions. Get a watch with a second hand. See how many good sits you can get in thirty seconds, then take a short break and start again. Of course, you'll have to encourage Mr. Sitting Pretty to get up after each repetition, to set him up for the next. Do this by backing up a bit and urging him toward you, or by tossing the treat a little bit away from him, so he has to get up to get it. After he's performing the sit reliably every time, add the verbal cue "Sit" *as he begins to sit.*

It has been theorized that canines have such acute hearing that they can hear a potato chip hit the carpet. They surely hear us saying "Sit"—so say it exactly once. Don't get into the habit of repeating cues. If your wolfdog doesn't sit the first time, either he doesn't understand the behavior well enough (in which case you need to back up a bit and start again), you didn't have his attention before you asked for the sit, or he has chosen not to do it. If the latter is the case, throw up your hands, say "Oh well," walk away and ignore him. No treat, no punishment, no big deal. Stop for a little while, then try again later.

A hand signal comes in handy (bad pun intended) when speaking is not possible or your wolfdog is at a distance. Begin with your arm hanging straight down by your side, palm facing forward. In a crisp, military-style move, bend your elbow, bringing your palm in toward you. The hand signal may be added once your wolfdog already knows the verbal cue for Sit. Give the hand signal first, then the verbal cue. Eventually, you can fade the verbal cue if you'd like.

As you continue training and your wolfdog really "gets it," begin to (click and) reward only for the best sits, i.e. the straightest or the fastest. But don't be stingy! You want to keep the game interesting, even as you reduce the number of rewards.

Once your wolfdog knows Sit, begin to work it into your daily routine. Ask him to sit for his meal, when having his leash clipped on for a walk, loading up into the car, getting petted, or getting a treat. In other words, ask him to sit before giving him anything he really wants. In those situations a food reward is unnecessary, as the reward is the meal, the petting, the walk, the car ride, etc.

Down, Boy!

Take a moment to consider which word you will use as a verbal cue for lying down. Be sure it's not the same word you use for other things. For example, a lot of folks, when their wolfdogs jump up on furniture or counters, admonish, "Down!" If this is the case in your home, use another cue such as "Drop" for lying down. Be sure that everyone in the family is consistent about which word is used for what.

Make teaching Down easier on yourself and your wolfdog by training it when he's tired. Begin with him in sitting, facing you. Position a treat just in front of your wolfdog's nose, then move it slowly (as though the treat were magnetized to his nose) *straight down to the ground* rather than toward yourself, which could cause your wolfdog to stand up to go after it. If that happens, don't say a word. Simply ask for another sit and start over. If he follows the treat into a full lying down position, click and give him the treat. If you are not using a clicker, simply say "Good boy!" Treat while he's still lying down.

Some wily woofers will try to get the treat with their rear still up in the air. If yours does, hold on to the treat and move it along the ground toward you. Did that draw him into a full down? If not, let him lick at the treat but not grab it. Most will eventually put their rear down. Alternately, you could shape the down by rewarding the raised-butt position, then in subsequent repetitions, rewarding a bit flatter positioning each time, until he's fully down.

Once your wolfdog catches on, try the luring motion without a treat in hand. (This sets the stage for the hand signal.) Once your wolfdog is lying down, (click and) treat from the other hand. You are already beginning to fade the food lure!

Following the lure to the ground...

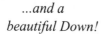

...and a beautiful Down!

If you still can not get your wolfdog to lie down, try this trick: Sit on the ground with one leg curled under and one leg extended out and slightly bent, so that your knee forms the top of a low archway. With your wolfdog on the outside of the arched leg, hold the treat a few inches away, on the other side. To get the treat, he will have to move his head under your leg, then part of his body, which will cause him to flatten into a lying down position. You may have to lure him by passing the treat closer to him then pulling it away, underneath your leg. If you are positioned correctly and hold on to the treat, he should lay completely down. When he does, (click and) praise, and give him the treat. Of course, if your wolfdog is a whole lot bigger than you are, this method may not be feasible. (Note: There is a good photo sequence of this method in Dr. Ian Dunbar's wonderful book, *How to Teach a New Dog Old Tricks* - see *Resources*.)

As with the Sit, you can capture the Down. Wait until your wolfdog is tired out, then go to a low-distraction area with him and wait, or turn on the television and go sit down yourself. He will more than likely lie down eventually. When he does, (click and) treat. Remember, that which is rewarded is likely to happen again, and in no time at all your wolfdog should be lying down and looking at you expectantly.

If all else fails, modeling can be used to teach the Down. With your wolfdog in a sitting position, place one arm under his two front legs, and rest the other lightly on his back. *Gently* swoop his front legs forward, keeping your hand on his back, lowering him into a Down. Don't forget the reward!

Once your wolfdog understands and is reliably performing the Down, add the verbal cue just as he starts lying down. Once that's established, add the hand signal if you'd like. It looks like this: palm down, hand moves toward the floor. As your wolfdog catches on, gradually make the hand signal less dramatic, so that eventually you are making a very small motion. Remember, hand signal first, then verbal cue.

Have your wolfdog practice sitting and then lying down, but practice sits without downs as well. Otherwise, you could end up with a wolfdog who anticipates and immediately goes into a Down each time you ask for a Sit. You can also lure your wolfdog up from a down, into a sit. Down, Sit, Down...in puppy class, we call these "puppy pushups."

Won't You Stay Just A Little Bit Longer...

Once your wolfdog knows Sit or Down, he can practice Stay in either position. Let's start with the Sit-Stay. Ask your wolfdog to sit, facing you. Without moving away, put your hand up with palm facing him as though you're saying "Halt." Instead, say "Stay." Don't put your hand right up to his nose, or he will likely get up to follow it (especially if it smells like yummy treats). Don't look stern. Smile! After all, he's doing what you've asked. Reward *during* the stay with a calm "Good boy" and a treat, making sure you extend the treat all the way to him so he doesn't have to get up for it. At first, do only a three second stay. Release him from the stay by saying, "Okay!" or whichever release word you have chosen. *Do not expect your wolfdog to sit for more than a few seconds at first.* One of the most common mistakes when teaching dogs to stay is to expect too much too soon. If three seconds is more than your wolfdog can handle at first, start with one second. As with everything else, raise the criteria in small increments, thereby setting your companion up to succeed. Once he's done a few successful repetitions of three-second stays, increase the time to five seconds, and so on.

With most behaviors, we give the command once and then we're quiet. With Stay, it's perfectly okay to help your wolfdog hold the position by using your voice. Once you've given the Stay command and hand signal, help him out by saying, "Goood boy, that's a goood stay" every few seconds in an even, soothing voice. Remember to smile and treat *during* the stay. At the end of your prescribed stay time, give the release word.

193

If your wolfdog breaks the stay, *that's* when you give the stern look. Get him back into sitting position, give the Stay cue, and start smiling! Realize too that if he's broken the stay, you've asked for too much too soon. Start over, going back to a shorter duration.

Once your wolfdog has a solid 60-second Sit-Stay right next to you, begin to add distance. Ask him to stay (using the hand signal as well), then take a step away. Drop the time you expect him to stay back to five seconds. Build slowly and don't expect too much too soon. (Don't go out for coffee and expect Timber to be sitting there when you get back.) Gradually increase the distance by taking two steps away and so on, dropping the time back down to five seconds with each added step, building from there before moving further. Don't push it, and don't move too far too fast. Your patience will pay off, and you will end up with a wolfdog with a solid Stay.

While your wolfdog is learning this behavior, be sure that you end the Stay by *going to your wolfdog to release him*, rather than calling him back to you. If you call him to you every time, you'll end up with a wolfdog who tensely waits for your recall rather than patiently sit-staying. Once he's got a reliable Stay as well as a reliable recall, you can change things up by calling him out of the Stay with a recall some of the time.

The Looong Down-Stay

One of the most wonderful things you can teach your wolfdog is a long down-stay. Some people prefer to use the word "Settle" for long down-stays, to let their wolfdog know he's going to be there a while.

Once your wolfdog is reliably performing down-stays, begin to gradually extend the "down time" until he will lay calmly for thirty minutes at a time. Practice at first with your wolfdog lying right near you, since it's easier for him that way. Watching television at night is the perfect time to practice this. As with the sit-stay, once you've built up duration, start increasing your distance from him. Do at least one long down-stay per day. This gives you both some well-deserved rest and is also wonderful for enforcing leadership.

Remember to practice all of these exercises in sessions spread throughout the day. Once your wolfdog understands them, begin to incorporate the behaviors into your daily routine. Now Sit, Stay, and read on...

Understanding Canine Body Language and Signals

Pop quiz: What does it mean when your wolfdog wags his tail?

> a. He's happy or excited
> b. He's stressed or anxious
> c. Either of the above

If you answered a, you are in the majority. Most canine owners have been taught that a wagging tail equals a happy dog. The correct answer, however, is c. A tail held parallel to the floor, swaying loosely from side to side in a wide arc, *is* most likely attached to a happy canine. But a tail held higher than usual, moving in a stiff, small arc (like a flag waving) is more likely attached to a canine who is anxious or showing dominance. In our household, it is usually attached to Mojo. We have dubbed it the "Cocky Tail." It is usually seen when he has something Soko wants (the "Make My Day" Cocky Tail), or is engaged in one of his displays of bully bravado (the "Forgot I Was Neutered" Cocky Tail). A tail held high can also signify confidence. Of course, we must take into consideration not only the position of each individual body part, but the sum of all visible signals, the body's overall posture, movements and vocalizations.

Soliciting play from a cocky-tailed boy.

Feelings, Aaarooo Feelings...

When Barry Manilow sings *Feelings*, he uses gestures and vocalizations to put across the emotion of the song. As most wolfdogs don't gesture or sing like Barry (thank goodness for small favors), we must make it a point to notice and understand canine body language. Developing this fluency will give you invaluable insight into how your wolfdog is feeling; and that can be crucial in influencing his interactions with other animals and people. It will allow you to understand the difference between rough play and actual fighting, and to recognize stress signals, thereby preventing potential harm to people and trauma to your wolfdog.

Wolves have an extremely clear line of communication with each other. Body language, vocalizations (i.e. howls, growls, whines), marking (i.e. raised leg urination on territorial boundaries or objects they consider theirs) and signals are used so clearly that disagreements seldom escalate into full-blown physical altercations. Though many modern dog breeds have diminished drives (i.e. prey drive) and certainly have a different appearance than that of their lupine ancestors, the communication they share has not become significantly diluted over the years. Even dogs with no wolf in them still show aggression, fear, affection and a range of other emotions through the same subtle alterations in ear, tail, mouth and body position used by wolves.

Just When You Think You Have the Answers...

Unfortunately, canine body language and behavior is easy to misinterpret. Many people, when watching two canines play wrestle, assume that the one lying on its back is the lower-ranking. It ain't necessarily so. Even the alpha in a wolf pack may play at mock submission with lower-ranking members. Another common misconception has to do with canines licking their owners on the mouth. Most owners assume it's because their fur-kid loves them. Of course they do, and licking on the mouth can be a sign of affection. But did you know that licking at another canine's (or person's) mouth is more often a submissive gesture? Pups do it to adult wolves to beg them to regurgitate a meal. (No, you don't need to lose your lunch!) Licking at another wolf's mouth can be a greeting behavior as well.

Monty Sloan of Wolf Park describes a particular bit of body language which is easily misconstrued: "There is an expression called an antagonistic pucker. A wolf with this expression has its lips retracted, baring its canines and incisors. It may or may not be doing other things: It may have its tail up or down, its ears forward or back, it may be crouching or it may be standing up tall. Looking at the other signals the wolf is giving, an observer can get a clearer picture of what the antagonistic pucker signal means. A puckering wolf which is also crouching with its tail down and its ears back is probably frightened and defensive; it is being submissive but warning that it will fight if pressed. A puckering wolf which has its tail up

and its ears forward and is standing tall is probably self-confident and is trying to do something like guard food from another wolf."

Perhaps the most misunderstood canine body language involves what is loosely termed "aggression." A wolfdog walking on leash who growls, snarls, or lunges with hackles up at passing canines is obviously not happy to see them. But does it mean he wants to do them bodily harm? Not necessarily. Many canines "display" in this way because they are actually *afraid* of the other dog. It's their way of saying *"Stay away from me, you Big Scary Thing, or I'll have to hurt you! Yeah, that's it, stay right where you are. Or better yet, leave!"* Many owners' first impulse is to jerk the leash or otherwise correct their wolfdogs when this happens, which (as described in *Fear Issues*) actually makes the problem worse.

It is can be difficult to get an accurate read on body language when it happens quickly and changes rapidly. As Barry Lopez writes in *Of Wolves and Men*, "Many encounters are simple, but it would be misleading to establish simplicity of gesture as the rule. An obviously 'submissive' wolf may be expressing submission, fear, and defensive aggression simultaneously. Even trained ethologists have mistaken who the submissive animal in an encounter was, thinking that an inhibited bite (a submissive gesture) was an attack (a display of dominance)." Well, since we do have to start somewhere, keeping Lopez's cautions in mind, let's look at the most obvious canine body language:

Calm: Relaxed tail, ears and mouth, no tension in body.

Dominance: Erect stance, tail waving stiffly and held high, back legs spread, body stiff, hackles may be up (piloerection), body may appear puffed up to appear larger, ears forward, hard stare. May use postures/gestures such as body slams, standing over or straddling another animal, "humping" another animal, clamping another's muzzle between one's teeth, placing paw over another's back or shoulders, walking stiffly.

Aggression: Raised hackles, tail lifted higher, lips pulled back to show teeth. Leans forward, snarls. Jaw squared, nostrils and pupils dilated. (Note that raised hackles are a sign of arousal, but not always a sign of aggression. Many canines raise hackles during play or when excited.)

Fear: Ears back, tail dropped and possibly tucked, entire body held lower to the ground. Head lowers in relation to neck. Hackles may be raised. Lip-line becomes loose; may drool. Eyebrows arched, brow furrowed. No teeth exposed. May whine.

Submission: Flattened body, flattened ears. Tail held low, may wag in small, stiff motion. Grovels, displays appeasement gestures such as licking, raised paw, may roll on back and present inguinal region and/or neck, may urinate.

Completely overwhelmed: Body completely flattened to the ground, eyes averted, may urinate.

Play: Easily recognizable "play bow;" hindquarters raised, elbows on floor, tail usually wagging. Direct eye contact, ears perked. May be "grinning." May try to engage another in play by pawing at them.

Stalking: Though more of a behavior than a body posture, no discussion of wolfdog body language would be complete without the inclusion of stalking. Wolves are cat-like when they stalk. Head lowered, back flat and low to the ground, ears up and tail wagging (yes, tail wagging!), tension in the body. There is complete silence and a sense of stealth; total focus. The walk is slow and deliberate. If you haven't seen this behavior in your wolfdog, you may have seen it in your cat. Wolfdogs have been known to show predatory behavior when following birds, cats, other small animals and even children. At Wolf Park in Indiana, when the captive wolves follow visiting children back and forth along the fence line, it is most often stalking behavior.

An interesting point regarding the media's portrayal of wolves displaying stalking behavior, from Monty Sloan of Wolf Park: "Some documentaries show hunting wolves growling or snarling at their prey with their hackles raised. Wolves do not do this. Growling and snarling are part of social aggression, expressions of an intention to fight, used between wolves. Wolves do not growl or snarl at their prey. It would be like a human getting angry at an ice cream cone he or she was about to eat! Wolves who are hunting look very excited and happy, even 'friendly'. Their tails wag, their ears are up, and they are quiet. They stare at their prey and look very focused."

Playing at dominance and submission

Happy, calm, relaxed!

Fearful - note the body tension

Let's play!

Calming Signals

Wolf biologists refer to "cutoff signals." These are messages, sent via posturing and facial expression, to let others know that the one signaling does not mean harm. They are also a canine way of "crying uncle." Cutoff signals diffuse aggressive situations before they escalate, thereby keeping peace in the pack. Until Norwegian dog trainer and author Turid Rugaas wrote *On Talking Terms With Dogs: Calming Signals*, most people were not aware that canines of all types use these signals regularly.

Rugaas explains that calming signals are not only a means to conflict resolution, but can prevent conflicts from happening in the first place: "The signals are used at an early state to prevent things from happening, avoiding threats from people and dogs, calming down nervousness, fear, noise and unpleasant things. The signals are used for calming themselves when they feel stressed or uneasy. The signals are used to make the others involved feel safer and understand the goodwill the signals tell about. They are used to make friends with other dogs and people."

> Calming signals give us invaluable information about how our wolfdogs are feeling. One of the best things about them is that once we are aware of them, we can actually use the signals ourselves, to calm our canine companions!

Though Rugaas outlines 28 basic signals, most are not usable by us, for either physical reasons (that pesky not having a tail thing) or social reasons (do you really want to play-bow on a busy street?)

Here are a few easily recognizable calming signals that we can make use of:

Yawning - We all know that canines yawn when they're tired. But you might be surprised at how often they yawn when stressed. I've seen training classes where a dog would yawn repeatedly. The owner would inevitably joke, "I think he's getting bored." The truth is, their dog was probably getting frustrated with the way they were training or stressed by something in the environment. Yawning is one of the signals we can easily identify and use ourselves. If your wolfdog is stressed, give a big, exaggerated yawn while he's looking  at you. He may respond in kind, or visibly calm. Individual canines vary in their level of response to calming signals.

Lip Licking - A quick, often repetitive licking of the lower lip. Ever take a photo of your wolfdog, where it looks like he's sticking his tongue out at you? Many wolfdogs are stressed by things such as cameras pointing directly at them, and so they throw calming signals like lip-licking. The signal is quick, but you can easily learn to spot it. We can use lip-licking as well, though it probably falls in the category of "things to use with discretion in public."

Turning Away - This is a great one that I use frequently to put nervous wolfdogs at ease, especially upon first meeting. In the canine world, turning the body, head or gaze away indicates that we are not a threat. It can also say, "Don't hurt me" to another canine who is displaying aggressive behavior. (Turning away is another signal you may notice when trying to photograph your wolfdog.) With nervous wolfdogs, crouch down and turn your body slightly to one side. Don't make eye contact, and keep your movements slow, your voice low and soothing (or don't talk at all). You'll appear much less threatening.

When two canines meet, they approach each other in an arc, rather than head-on. That gives them a chance to check out each others' body language before getting up close and personal. It also gives one or both the chance to calm the other by turning the head and/ or body away. When you walk your wolfdog on leash, try to avoid approaching another canine nose-to-nose, straight on.

Turning away from the camera and licking lips.

Other calming signals which are easily noticeable are scratching oneself (definitely in the not-for-use-in-public category!) and sniffing the ground. Sure, these two occur for a variety of reasons anyway; but they are most definitely used when canines feel stressed. I compare these particular signals to things we do when passing someone on the street who makes us nervous, or having a conversation with someone who is making us feel uncomfortable. In those circumstances, as a nervous reaction, I tend to look at my watch (looking away). Some women might nervously brush a strand of hair back from their face. A man might straighten his tie or clear his throat. These are all "calming signals" too, and I'll bet we use them more than we realize. The scratching and sniffing are no different for dogs. I have often noticed my German Shepherd Soko developing a sudden itch at the sight of Mojo's "cocky tail."

Always remember that to convey calm to your wolfdog, you must remain calm yourself. It's amazing how sensitive canines are to our facial expressions, body language, and the tension present in our body. If you relax, breathe, move slowly and speak calmly, you'll have a much better chance of calming a stressed canine.

Begin to pay attention to calming signals in your wolfdog. Watch carefully when he interacts with other canines, and notice what the others do in response. Monitor for calming signals during training sessions, so you'll know whether your wolfdog is getting stressed. Pay special attention when he uses calming signals around other people; perhaps that person makes him nervous. Once you really start picking up on body language and calming signals, it's like a new world has opened up. You'll gain a whole new level of understanding of your companion, and a great way to communicate with him.

Veterinary Care

This chapter was generously contributed by Diane Delbridge, D.V.M. The information presented, as with all information in this book, is not meant to take the place of proper veterinary care. If you suspect your wolfdog is ill, consult your veterinarian.

Immunity: How Vaccines Work
Diseases Preventable by Vaccination
Typical Vaccine Schedules
Rabies and Wolfdogs
Taking Your Wolfdog to the Vet
Home Care
Spaying and Neutering
Signs of Disease
Canine Bloat
Heartworms/Hookworms/Roundworms/
Whipworms/Tapeworms
Coccidia
Giardia

Immunity: How Vaccines Work

When a person or an animal is exposed to a disease-causing germ such as a bacterium or a virus, several defense mechanisms go into action to recognize the germ as foreign and to eliminate it. A very important role is played in this process by antibodies. These are proteins in the bloodstream which are programmed to recognize a specific germ and attach to it, "flagging" it for killing by the body's defensive cells, the white blood cells. Antibodies are only present in the bloodstream if the body created them following previous exposure to this same germ. (The only exception is in the very young when there are maternal antibodies made by the mother and given to the puppy through the milk.) It takes about seven days after a first exposure to a germ for the body to create new antibodies. On subsequent exposures, antibodies can be replicated much quicker, and can often overwhelm the attacking germs before they can cause disease symptoms.

The purpose of a vaccine, then, is to provide that first exposure to a germ and stimulate antibody production, so that subsequent exposures can be fought off without disease occurring. Since we don't want disease to occur on the first exposure either, the germs that are put into vaccines are first changed in some way so that they still stimulate the immune system but they cannot produce disease. Some vaccines are called "killed" because the germ is dead, such as rabies vaccines. Some are called "modified live" because the virus is still alive but altered to make it weaker. A newer type of vaccine is called a "sub-unit vaccine," where only the part of the germ that stimulates the immune system is included in the vaccine.

Now let's go back to the pup with its maternal antibodies. These antibodies are going to recognize the vaccine germ and get rid of it so quickly that the pup's own immune system doesn't have time to identify the substance as foreign and start to make antibodies against it. So the vaccine has failed to stimulate immunity in this case. The only way the pup will make its own antibodies to the vaccine is when there are no longer enough maternal antibodies to get to all the vaccine germs first. This is why puppies are given a series of vaccinations at regular intervals: because every pup runs out of maternal antibodies at a different time, and we want to get a vaccine response as soon as possible after that before the pup contacts the real thing.

Whenever we give a second or additional vaccine for the same germ it is called a "booster shot." This is because the second exposure to the germ boosts the original response and creates even more antibodies than the first shot did. Some germs are not very good at stimulating an immune response, and boosters are very important to ensure that sufficient antibodies are present. Other germs create a much bigger response, and boosters may not be needed as often.

Diseases Preventable by Vaccination

Although some people would have you believe otherwise, wolves and wolfdogs get the very same diseases and take the very same shots that other dogs do. Data gathered in 1998 and 1999 and submitted to the USDA has shown that wolves and wolfdogs are no more likely to have adverse reactions to vaccinations than other dogs. There are *no known incidences* of live vaccine virus causing the actual diseases in wolves.

Canine Distemper is a relatively common disease of puppies and young adults, and is caused by a virus. It is passed from one dog to another through nasal and ocular (eye) secretions, sneezing and coughing, and via the urine and feces. About four days after exposure, dogs develop a fever, runny eyes and nose, and lethargy. The fever usually subsides after two to three days, then returns a few days later. The dog will then develop vomiting, diarrhea, and coughing, which often signals pneumonia. Some dogs develop pustules on their skin and hardening of the paw pads. Some dogs also develop neurological signs including muscle tics, difficulty walking, and sometimes grand mal seizures. Those that get only the "head cold" symptoms may recover. The prognosis is worse if neurological signs appear. Many dogs that do recover from distemper have seizure disorders later in life.

Canine distemper virus is closely related to the measles virus. Measles virus was once used to try to overcome maternal antibodies in young pups. This practice has fallen in disfavor with the advent of the newer vaccines. Canine distemper virus can be killed using most disinfectants, and doesn't survive long in the environment.

Canine Infectious Hepatitis is caused by a virus called canine adenovirus type 1. It is also seen in puppies and young dogs, and causes an often-fatal liver disease. Due to liver failure, the affected dog may have a swollen abdomen, vomiting and diarrhea, and skin and internal bleeding. Symptoms usually develop six to nine days after exposure via direct contact (licking and mouthing), or by ingestion of urine or feces of affected dogs. This virus survives outside the host animal for weeks or months, and should be killed using 1/4 strength bleach (one part bleach mixed with three parts water).

Leptospirosis is caused by a spiral-shaped bacterium that lives mostly in ponds, rivers and sewage lagoons. The bacteria are transmitted to dogs through infected drinking water, coming in contact with the mucous membranes of the eyes or genitals, or by penetrating into a cut or wound. Thus dogs normally get lepto by swimming in, playing in, or drinking water from a pond or river. These bacteria can cause three different clinical syndromes: an acute bleeding disease, a liver disease with severe jaundice, or kidney failure. There are several varieties of this bacteria that affect dogs, and we normally vaccinate against two of the most common ones. Unfortunately, many of the recent cases across the U.S. have been from different varieties than what is in the vaccine. In addition, the lepto fraction of the vaccine seems to be the most likely to cause facial swelling and itching after vaccination, so many veterinarians are no longer including lepto in their routine vaccine protocols. This will vary in different regions of the country, so ask your veterinarian.

Parainfluenza is a virus, bordatella is a bacterium, and they are the two most common organisms causing "kennel cough" in dogs. Both are passed through coughing or nose-to-nose contact. About four to seven days after exposure, dogs will develop a dry honking cough, which is often followed by gagging. Symptoms may run their course in five to seven days, or they may persist for three to four weeks. Once infected, dogs often relapse periodically. The disease is called kennel cough because it is usually transmitted in places where there are a lot of dogs such as kennels, humane societies, grooming shops and dog shows. Vaccine against parainfluenza is usually incorporated into the "7-in-1" yearly vaccinations. Bordatella can be given in an injectable form, though there is a vaccine which combines the two germs into one shot, which is dripped into the nose. This type of vaccine works by causing "local immunity"—in this case antibodies which form in the nasal passages—where they will be ready to go to work if the germs are inhaled.

Parvovirus is a frequently fatal disease of puppies. It is transmitted through the feces of infected dogs, but can also be carried from an infected area to your home or yard on contaminated toys or feeding utensils, on shoes, and by flies. Five to seven days after exposure, puppies will suddenly become lethargic, stop eating, run a fever, and drool or tremble from abdominal cramps. They will soon begin severe vomiting a have very runny diarrhea which contains large amounts of blood. Many die within just a day or two of severe dehydration and opportunistic bacterial infection. Some can be saved with prompt treatment. This virus can live several months in the yard or on floors, and cannot be killed with most household cleaners. A 1:16

dilution of chlorine bleach must be used (one part bleach to 16 parts water). Because of the high mortality of this disease, there is much ongoing research into effective vaccines. In recent years, a new type of vaccine called "high-titer" has been developed which seems to protect more puppies from parvo at a slightly younger age.

Coronavirus is similar to parvo in that it can cause vomiting and diarrhea. However, the symptoms are not as severe as with parvo. There is some controversy whether corona causes disease by itself, or if it only occurs simultaneously with parvovirus. Some "7-in-1" vaccines also include this virus.

Lyme Disease is caused by spirochete bacteria much like lepto. In this case the bacteria is transmitted to dogs by the bite of the deer tick, and other ticks in some areas of the U.S. This disease has been seen sporadically in the U.S., being much more common in some areas than in others. Ask your veterinarian whether the disease is common enough in your area to warrant vaccination. Lyme disease causes fever, lethargy, joint pain, swollen lymph nodes, and anemia. It is important to note that people can get the same disease from the same ticks, but dogs and people do not transmit the disease directly to one another. Be careful when picking ticks off your dog and wash well afterwards. Ticks should be prevented on dogs by Preventic Collars or Frontline Top Spot, and by spraying of the environment when feasible.

Typical Vaccination Schedules

The goal of puppy vaccinations is to stimulate an immune response soon after the pup's maternal antibodies drop too low. Since we don't know exactly when that is, we usually give puppies a series of shots to be certain that proper immunity is achieved. It is important to remember that vaccinations should only be given to *healthy* puppies. If a pup's immune system is already busy fighting off an illness, it will not respond properly to a vaccine. Also remember that a pup's immune system is not fully functional until somewhere around five or six weeks of age, so vaccinations given prior to this age may not work. There are also many other factors which can affect how well a vaccine works, such as nutrition, internal parasites, environmental stresses, proper handling of the vaccine, and proper administration of the shot.

The goal of annual adult vaccinations is to boost the dog's antibody levels so that it is constantly ready to fight off disease. Most vaccinations that are given to puppies are boostered every year. Many studies are currently under way to determine if yearly revaccination is really necessary for all the common diseases, or if immunity actually lasts longer than that. Studies have already been done on rabies vaccine and some brands of this vaccine are licensed to be given every three years instead of yearly.

Other conditions must be considered for adult dog vaccinations. Dogs should not be vaccinated while they are pregnant. Dogs that are being given cortisone products for allergic conditions must have their dosage schedule altered at vaccination time, since the point of the cortisone is to suppress the immune response. Dogs that are being treated for cancer or autoimmune disease will also be immunosuppressed and should not be vaccinated. And we must remember that chronic diseases in older dogs such as heart failure or kidney failure will stress their bodies enough to make their immune systems less effective, making yearly boosters even more important.

The following is an example of a typical vaccination schedule. This may need to be modified in different geographical areas depending on disease prevalence and local laws. Please ask your veterinarian what is recommended in your area.

Puppies: Distemper, Hepatitis, Parainfluenza and Parvovirus (DHPP or DA2PP) are given at 6, 9, 12 and 15 weeks of age. If high-titer vaccine is used, the 15-week shot may not be needed. If a pup is not started on time, at least two vaccinations must be given three weeks apart, with the second at or after 12 weeks of age. Lepto and/or corona may be included with these vaccines. For puppies that are going to be shown, kenneled, or groomed, intranasal Bordatella can be given in a single dose at the 9 or 12 week vaccination, and should be repeated every six months if the dog continues to be exposed. Lyme disease vaccine, if needed, is given at 9 and 12 weeks of age. Rabies is given once between 12 and 16 weeks of age.

Adults: Yearly boosters of DA2PP, with or without lepto are given, and Lyme disease shots in affected areas. Rabies is given at one year past the puppyhood shot (i.e. at 16 months), and thereafter either yearly or every three years, depending on local laws.

Rabies and Wolfdogs

Rabies is a virus that causes a progressive, fatal neurological disease in dogs, cats, humans, raccoons, foxes, skunks, horses, cattle, bats, ferrets, and many other mammals. In various regions of the U.S. there are wild carrier species—usually skunks, raccoons, or foxes—that harbor the virus and pass it on to domestic animals. Domestic animals, in turn, can pass it on to humans through close contact. When an animal is bitten by an infected carrier, the virus transmits from the saliva of the sick animal into the bite wound of the victim. The virus then travels along the nerves to the brain where it multiplies, then spreads via other nerves to the salivary glands, where it can then be transmitted to another animal. Initial symptoms of rabies are unusual behavioral changes, such as active animals becoming sullen and withdrawn ("dumb form"), or quiet animals becoming fearless and aggressive ("furious form"). It progresses to paralysis of the throat and facial muscles, which makes the animal unable to swallow. (The resulting drooling often causes owners to examine their pet's mouth, thereby exposing the person to the virus.) Paralysis of the entire body follows rapidly. Sometimes seizures occur, and death comes soon after. Diagnosis can only be confirmed by microscopic examination of brain tissue.

In the U.S., there has long been a controversy over vaccination of wolves and wolfdogs against rabies virus. In years past, when modified live rabies vaccine was sometimes used, scientists feared that the live virus would "revert" to its original deadly form in a "wild animal;" so it was not given to wolves. Now that we only use the killed virus vaccine, this is no longer a concern. However, none of the killed virus vaccines have ever been approved by the USDA for use in wolves or wolfdogs, and this creates several problems. One problem is that wolfdog owners may be unable to find a veterinarian who is legally allowed to vaccinate their pet for rabies, thus the animal may go unvaccinated and thereby be susceptible to rabies. This endangers not only the wolfdog but also any humans it comes into contact with. Another problem is that even if the veterinarians in your state are allowed to vaccinate your wolfdog, the animal is still considered "wild" if it bites someone, no matter the circumstances, and it is euthanized and tested for rabies. Because of this "catch-22" situation, many wolfdog owners call their pets a Malamute mix, Shepherd mix, or whatever type of dog it most resembles, in order to get it legally vaccinated for rabies. Yet another problem with having no approved rabies vaccine is that many states, counties, and other legal jurisdictions use this as an excuse to outlaw ownership of wolves and wolfdogs.

The fight for approval of the rabies vaccine for wolves and wolfdogs has been going on for several years. In the past, wolves and dogs were classified as different species, *Canis lupus* and *Canis familiaris*. But in 1993, taxonomists reclassified dogs as a subspecies of wolves, calling dogs *Canis lupus familiaris*. This is important because the rabies vaccine is approved by the USDA for an entire species at a time, such as all breeds of cats, or all breeds of cattle. With the reclassification, it would seem that wolves and wolfdogs should be approved under the existing licenses for canine vaccines. But despite the recommendation of such an approval by a panel of scientists and experts in 1998, the USDA *still* did not change its regulations. Instead, data was collected from zoos and veterinarians who were already vaccinating wolves and wolfdogs in their care, to determine whether these vaccines were causing any harmful reactions in these animals. In 1999, after reviewing this data, the USDA proposed a rule change that would classify wolves and wolfdogs as the same species as dogs with regard to licensing of vaccines.

This rule change is still being debated.

Here are the main things wolfdog owners need to know about rabies: First, rabies vaccine (and other common canine vaccines) will work on your pet, and it is very important that he be vaccinated. Second, you may have to identify your wolfdog as a canine mix, avoiding the word "wolf," to get him legally vaccinated. Third, if you don't identify your wolfdog as anything but an ordinary dog, in the event of a bite, he should be quarantined for 10 days like any other dog and not euthanized for rabies testing. Fourth, laws vary from state to state as to whether veterinarians are allowed to vaccinate a wolfdog. Some recommend it, some prohibit it, and some make no distinction between wolfdogs and other dogs. Find out what the laws are in your area. Fifth, there are federal ruling changes pending which should make getting legal vaccinations much easier in the future.

Taking Your Wolfdog to the Vet

Taking a large canine to a veterinary clinic can be scary for the dog and harrowing for the people. This can be even worse if your wolfdog is not good at car travel, is apprehensive in new situations, is afraid of new people, or is aggressive toward other animals. Ideally, many of these problems could be avoided by socializing your new puppy early in life (see *Socialization*). Also remember that many vets are willing to help you get your pup comfortable with their clinic and their staff by having you drop in for pet-and-treat visits. Be sure to ask for their help if your pup seems scared at their office. If you have an adult wolfdog that already has some of these problems, be sure to alert the staff when you make the appointment. They may be able to schedule you when the clinic is quiet, in order to avoid crowds. They may also be able to accommodate your choice of male or female doctors and staff if

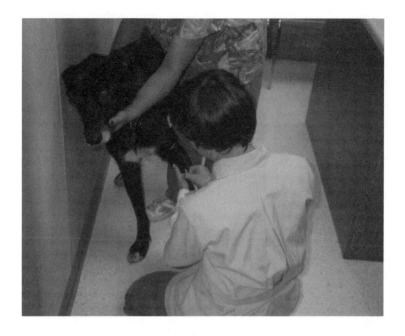

your wolfdog is, for example, afraid of men or aggressive towards women. Be sure to tell them if there are certain procedures that your wolfdog will not allow, such as temperature-taking or toenail-trimming. If your wolfdog truly becomes unmanageable at the vet's office, discuss with them the possibility of giving tranquilizers to your pet before bringing him to the clinic. Keep in mind that a tranquilizer must be given to an animal that is not already highly agitated for it to work properly. A high percent wolfdog, for instance, that has already become excited by attempts to load into the car, will not slow down much when tranquilized. This can lead to a dangerous situation if the choice is made to give more tranquilizer, because the adrenaline rush will still counteract it. Then hours later, when the animal has a chance to calm down on his own, he may become overly sedated as the medication finally takes effect. Also remember that acepromazine, a commonly used tranquilizer, has a wide dosage range and highly variable effects from dog to dog. Some wolfdogs need very little while some need a whole lot, so it is best to start with a low dose until you know how that particular animal is affected.

If you are going to a vet who doesn't know you and your wolfdogs, it may be best not to tell anyone your dog is part wolf. This is especially true in states where wolfdogs are illegal to own, because the vet may not be able to legally treat your pet and still be covered by insurance. There are very few medications or procedures for which the vet needs to know that your animal is part wolf, so it would not make a difference in the way his condition is treated.

Besides the issues with the initial exam, there are other situations about your relationship with your wolfdog that you may need to discuss with your vet when deciding on treatment for a particular illness. If he has an eye condition, can you apply drops three times daily? If he has an ear infection, can you clean his ears and apply ointment twice daily? If he has a lameness that requires rest, can you confine him to prevent running and jumping for seven to ten days? Can you give him a pill two or three times per day, or would once-daily medication be asking a lot? Is it okay to give the prescribed medicine with food, if that is the only way to get him to take it? If he needs to be hospitalized, will he allow staff to handle him and will he stay in his kennel? Remember that if you get your puppy accustomed to having his eyes, ears, teeth, feet, etc. handled at a young age, medicating should be much easier later on. No matter how sound a treatment plan your vet devises, it won't work if you can't carry it out.

Home Care and First Aid

There are many aspects of your wolfdog's veterinary care that take place at home. These include routine grooming and inspection, first aid for emergencies, and carrying out a medication or treatment plan in case of illness or injury. *The keys to overall health for your pet are good nutrition, plenty of exercise, lots of love and attention, and early detection of problems so that molehills don't become mountains.*

In the course of your daily interactions with your pets, you become familiar with each one's habits, attitudes and quirks. And in the course of petting and grooming, you learn to recognize their scars, warts and bald spots. Familiarization is important because it allows you to notice when something has changed. Things you may notice include lethargy, change in appetite, change in bathroom habits, change in interaction with packmates, new lumps or bumps, hair loss, or unusual odors or discharges. There may also be more overt signs of a problem such as limping, vomiting or diarrhea, bleeding, coughing, or labored breathing. It is important that you notice both the subtle and the obvious so you can detect changes early and provide your vet with as many clues as possible to help him diagnose the problem.

Have a well-stocked first aid kit on hand. Be sure everyone in the family knows where it is and how to use it; replace what you use immediately so it is there for the next emergency. Take it or a special travel kit with you when traveling with your wolfdog. Remember to keep the number for the vet or emergency clinic close to the phone so you can call for advice before administering medications. There are some good books on the market on pet first aid, as well as courses through the American Red Cross. Do your research now so you're prepared if an emergency happens.

BE PREPARED! *A FIRST AID KIT SHOULD INLUDE:*

Latex gloves, muzzle or nylon stockings, nylon leash, gauze pads of various sizes, 2-inch-wide roll gauze, vet wrap or similar bandage, splint material such as sticks or cardboard, adhesive tape, non-adherent "telfa" pads, scissors, tweezers, needle nose pliers, safety pins, matches, "instant heat" and "instant cold" packs, compact thermal blanket, towel, rectal thermometer, penlight, 3% hydrogen peroxide, rubbing alcohol, Epsom salts, sterile eye lubricant, sterile eye wash, eye dropper, styptic powder or pencil, Benadryl, Vaseline, expired credit card to scrape away stingers, clean cloth, and a list of emergency numbers for your vet, the emergency vet clinic and poison control. For traveling, add paper towels and trash bags. You may want to buy an inexpensive tool box to store all this in, and clearly label the outside.

Home care of an ill or injured animal may be simple or complex. Make sure you understand how and when to give all medications, and whether they are to be used only for a few days or if they are going to be required permanently. If your pet is on any permanent medications, be sure you have someone who can give these if an emergency or vacation takes you away from home. Make a list of them and what they are for, and always have at least a few days' supply on hand. If your pet is bedridden for any length of time, be sure he is well padded, and turn him from side to side every few hours to prevent bedsores. Clean up any accidents right away to prevent urine scalding or stool caking. You may need to hand feed and water an immobilized pet. If there are any stitches or wounds, clean them daily as directed by your vet. Keep bandages or splints clean and dry, and check daily to see that they aren't too tight or too loose. And don't forget to return to your vet for scheduled rechecks, suture or bandage removals, or follow-up testing.

Spaying and Neutering: Should You?

For the great majority of wolfdog owners, breeding should not be an option. There are already way more wolfdogs who need homes than there are knowledgeable owners. Here are some of the points to consider if you are thinking of breeding your wolfdog: It is best to breed wolfdogs of verified ancestry. You should be able to document the percentage of wolf in your breeding pair through a reputable registry, so that you know exactly what you have and what you will be creating, percentage-wise.

Know what dog breeds are involved in your breeding pair, and use only those which compliment the wolf characteristics. The breeds most commonly bred with wolves are malamutes, huskies and shepherds. These breeds most resemble the wolf in looks and temperament. One should not use aggressive breeds such as Pit Bulls or Rottweilers.

Mature intact wolfdogs, especially high percenters, can become more aggressive than normal during breeding season. This is known as Winter Wolf Syndrome (*turn to chapter W to read more on this - NW*), and it can be avoided by spaying and neutering.

Good homes are hard to find for wolfdog pups, and bad homes are not only bad for the individual pup, but give all wolfdog owners a black eye. If you are going to breed, you must screen potential buyers carefully to be sure they know what they are getting into and that they have the proper knowledge and environment to care for a wolfdog. You should have several buyers lined up before even breeding, so that there are no unwanted pups. You will have to be available for questions and problems that the new owners encounter, long after they have taken the pups home. You should be willing to take the pups back should they not work out—after all, *you* created them, so *you* are ultimately responsible.

You should have your breeding pair screened for hip dysplasia to be sure you don't pass it on to the pups. Hip dysplasia is a condition in which the ball-and-socket joint of one or both hips is shaped poorly, leading to excessive movement of the ball within the socket, which is painful. In severe cases, the ball may fall out of the socket. Dogs with this disease require lifelong medication, surgery, or both, in order to be comfortable. Many dog breeds commonly mixed with wolves have a tendency towards HD; only dogs with excellent or good hip conformation should be bred.

Advantages of Spay/Neutering

Dogs that are spayed or neutered are less likely to fight, especially with members of the same sex. They are also less likely to try to escape their yard or pen in order to breed. Dogs that escape are not only a nuisance to the neighbors, but they are in danger of being hit by cars or being shot or getting into other trouble. Female dogs that are spayed before their first heat are extremely unlikely to develop breast cancer later in life. They are also no longer subject to ovarian cancer, uterine cancer, or uterine infections, since these parts are removed. And no messy heat cycles!

Male dogs that are neutered when they are young are not only protected from testicular cancer (since the testicles are removed), but they are also much less likely to develop prostate infections, prostate tumors, and perianal tumors.

With all these things to consider, breeding is best left to those with health-screened, verified animals who have enough experience to properly screen, educate and support their buyers. In general, a spayed or neutered wolfdog makes a better pet.

Both males and females require general anesthesia for their procedures, but the surgery is a little more extensive in females, as it requires going into the abdomen. Females may need to stay overnight at the vet hospital. The entire reproductive tract is removed, unlike in humans, where the tubes that carry eggs or sperm are just tied off. Because the ovaries or testicles are removed, their hormone production also stops. Therefore, females no longer come into heat and males no longer have an interest in females. Another by-product of decreased hormones is decreased metabolism, so your wolfdog may need less food to prevent weight gain after his surgery. While there are some risks any time an animal is anesthetized and surgery is performed, spaying and neutering are considered routine procedures; and with today's newer anesthetics, the risk is minimal. Clearly the benefits outweigh the risks for a healthy young dog. So… Don't Litter!

Signs of Disease

As we discussed under Home Care, there are many signs of disease that an owner should watch for. Some of the more obvious signs include vomiting, diarrhea, difficult or frequent urination, limping, bleeding, open wounds, frequent scratching, difficulty breathing, seizures, hair loss, coughing, swelling, and discharge from the eyes, nose, ears, or genitals. Some of the less obvious signs include decreased appetite, increased water consumption, decreased activity, standing or sitting more slowly than normal, enlarged lymph nodes, skin growths, rash, weight loss, dental or periodontal disease, head tilt, and impaired hearing or vision. Appearance of any one of these signs on an infrequent basis may not signify an important health problem. We all sneeze, cough, itch, or feel lousy now and then. But repeated coughing or itching, lethargy of more than a day or two, or combinations of two or three different signs, are cause for concern and should prompt a call or visit to your vet. Wolves, wolfdogs and dogs get many of the same diseases and conditions that people get, especially as they get older. Many of these conditions, such as diabetes, heart disease, kidney failure, and some forms of cancer, can be controlled when detected early and properly treated. The trick is to watch your pet carefully without overreacting, and seek veterinary advice when you are uncertain. And remember that good nutrition and exercise are the cornerstones of good health.

Canine Bloat

Canine bloat, or gastric dilatation-volvulus (GDV), is a life-threatening condition of the stomach. It is seen mostly in large, deep-chested breeds of dogs such as Dobermans, German Shepherds, Great Danes, Irish Setters, and Saint Bernards. Any wolfdog that is large and has a narrow, deep chest can also be affected. GDV occurs when the stomach gets very full of food and gas. If the stomach swells enough, its contents have difficulty either passing through to the intestine, or being vomited back up. The distended stomach then rotates, cutting off not only outflow of the contents but also the blood circulation that feeds the stomach itself. In addition, the spleen can become entrapped in the torsion and its circulation compromised. After only a few minutes of obstructed circulation, parts of the stomach and spleen can die. As they do so, chemicals are released into the bloodstream that start a cascade of serious reactions in other organs, the worst of which is an arrhythmia in the heart. An affected dog can die of this arrhythmia in only a few minutes.

Signs of GDV appear very quickly and may include restlessness, abdominal pain, drooling, unproductive retching, and an obviously swollen abdomen. This will progress to shock, weakness, rapid heart rate, and rapid breathing. *This is not a condition that can be treated at home! Rapid presentation to a veterinarian or emergency clinic is necessary to save your pet!* Your veterinarian will attempt to pass a tube down the dog's throat into his stomach to try to empty the food and gas. If the stomach has already twisted, this will not be possible. The next option is to relieve the gas by inserting a needle through the abdominal wall into the stomach. The dog must be treated for shock and any arrhythmia present. As soon as the dog is stable, surgery is necessary to return the stomach to its proper position. Sometimes part of the stomach and/or spleen must be removed. An important part of surgery is then tacking the stomach wall to the inside of the abdominal wall so that it cannot twist again. Complications may still arise after surgery, and some dogs still die in the first few days afterwards.

Researchers at Purdue University have extensively studied this condition, and they have set forth recommendations that can decrease your dog's risk of bloating. Those dogs that eat fast, especially if they gulp a lot of air with their food, must be slowed down. This can sometimes be accomplished by putting large, inedible objects in the bowl that the dog has to eat around. It is also a good idea to feed a smaller quantity of food in two or three meals during the day. Do not allow your dog to exercise for at least an hour after a meal, and do not allow him to drink a large quantity of water before or after exercising. Do *not* use raised feeding bowls. Raising the height of the bowl was once thought to speed passage of the food through the digestive tract, but research has shown that a dog with a raised bowl is twice as likely to bloat. Other risk factors include increasing age and having a first-degree relative who has bloated. Thus the older your dog is, the more carefully his eating and exercise habits should be monitored. And if a littermate, half sibling, or parent has had a GDV, Purdue researchers suggest a more diligent watch. They also recommend against breeding your dog, to keep from producing more susceptible individuals.

Heartworms

Heartworms are worms that actually live inside a dog's heart. The adult worms there make babies that swim around in the bloodstream. A mosquito taking a blood meal ingests these, and they actually undergo a molt in the mosquito's stomach before being injected into another dog during another bite. After that it takes six full months for the larvae to reach the heart and grow up and start making babies in the new dog. The old way to detect heartworms was to find the babies in a drop of blood on the microscope, but that missed quite a few cases that weren't making many babies yet. The new tests can detect a protein from the surface of the heartworm at 5 to 5 1/2 months post-infection or later.

When heartworms are left untreated, they will clog up the inside of the heart so that the valves don't close properly. They also take up space that should be occupied by moving blood. These things combine to make the heart a less efficient pump, and eventually will lead to heart failure. Dogs do not usually show symptoms of heartworms until their heart begins to fail. Early symptoms include weight loss and coughing, and dogs eventually become lethargic, lose their appetite, and have difficulty breathing. In a few rare cases, the heartworms congregate in a major vein that leads into the heart, cutting off blood flow, and the dog will sicken and die within just a few hours.

Heartworms can be prevented. The first preventive, introduced in the 1970's and still available, was diethylcarbamazine citrate, or DEC. It prevents the larvae that were deposited by the mosquito from molting into their next stage. However, since this molt occurs in less than five days, the drug has to be given every day to be certain it is present at the right time. The newer preventives are ivermectin (Heartgard) and its close relative, milbemycin (Interceptor). These drugs can stop the development of two different stages of the larvae, so they only have to be given once monthly. Late in 1999 another monthly preventive was introduced called selemectrin (Revolution). This drug is applied topically to the skin between the shoulder blades and is then absorbed systemically, where it works similarly to its cousins, ivermectin and milbemycin. It is important to test your dog before starting preventive, unless he is started as a young pup. Most preventives on the market will cause a rapid kill of the baby worms, if they are present. This can cause a serious, sometimes fatal, allergic-type reaction in the dog. That is why we don't want to give heartworm preventive if we don't know for certain the dog is negative. In areas of the country where mosquitoes are present most or all of the year, preventive is given year-round. In the north, it is often stopped for the winter. Your vet can advise you what is recommended in your area.

The treatment for adult heartworms is an arsenic compound. Two drugs are available, thiacetarsemide (Caparsolate) and melarsomine (Immiticide). The former has been the standard for many years, but had to be given intravenously in 4 or 5 treatments. The latter is a new drug which can be given intramuscularly in only two treatments. However, the arsenic can be very toxic or fatal to the dog while it is being fatal to the heartworms. It is also very expensive. It adds new meaning to the phrase, "An ounce of prevention is worth a pound of cure!" And even worse than the drug for most owners is the fact that they have to keep their dog from running for *six weeks* while the heartworms are dying. Picture that with your pets for a moment... The dying worms, five to eight inches long and about half the diameter of spaghetti, are broken into tiny pieces by the white blood cells before they can be digested. If a dog takes off running and jars some of these worm pieces loose from his heart, they go directly to his lungs and become dozens of tiny emboli that block the blood/oxygen flow in the lungs. This can have fatal consequences.

Sometime after the drug is given to kill the adult heartworms, the baby heartworms must be killed so the dog is no longer a reservoir of infection for nearby mosquitoes. The drug most often given is ivermectin, the same as in Heartgard and Ivomec. Dogs are usually hospitalized to do this, because this can cause the same reaction as giving preventive to an untested dog. Four months later the dog is retested to be sure he no longer has adult heartworms.

Another important thing about testing and preventive: If you test the dog when he is apparently healthy, and he turns out positive, he is much more likely to survive the treatment than if you wait until he is losing weight and coughing to have him tested. At that point his heart will already be somewhat damaged, and the poor blood flow from a failing heart will take its toll on the kidneys and liver, the organs most likely to be affected by the arsenic.

Hookworms

Hookworms are one of the most common intestinal worms in dogs. They are tiny, only about 1/4 of an inch long, but they are very damaging. They have six large hooks in their mouths which they sink into the intestinal wall, then they feed on blood. They also frequently change sites along the wall, leaving the old wound bleeding. In this way they are responsible for significant blood loss, and puppies with heavy infestations can easily and quickly die of anemia. Hookworms make a lot of eggs which are passed in the stool and hatch into larvae in the soil. These larvae are either swallowed when a dog eats off the ground, or they penetrate the feet to gain entrance. (Note that they can also penetrate the bare feet of humans and migrate through the tissues, causing significant damage.) In addition, larvae can be passed from mother to pups via the milk. By whatever method they are obtained, the larvae migrate via the bloodstream to the lungs, where they are coughed up into the trachea and swallowed. They then molt into adults and begin to feed. The full cycle takes between two and three weeks. Hookworms can be treated with a number of different wormers, the most common being pyrantel pamoate (Strongid or Nemex), or as part of their monthly heartworm preventive with either Heartgard, Interceptor, or Revolution. Cleaning up stools from the yard before the eggs can hatch is an important step in preventing reinfection.

Roundworms

Roundworms are another common intestinal worm of dogs. They are four to seven inches long and nearly the diameter of spaghetti. These worms can clog up the intestine and consume significant amounts of nutrients that otherwise would nourish the dog. But even more damage is done by the larval stages on their migration through the body, because they migrate through the liver and lungs before being coughed up and swallowed. In adult dogs, many of these larvae never make the complete cycle, and wind up in various internal organs. In the case of pregnant female dogs, these larvae will "awaken" due to hormonal changes and migrate across the placenta into the lungs of the fetuses, and then migrate through the pups' tissues soon after birth. Pups already infected at birth take about three weeks to begin passing eggs, whereas dogs infected by swallowing eggs take four to five weeks. If a person, usually a child, swallows roundworm eggs, the larvae will migrate throughout their body, causing serious damage. Roundworms can be treated with the same medications that kill hookworms. In addition, piperazine is an older but effective treatment.

Whipworms

Whipworms are not as common as the other worms we have discussed. They live in the large intestine and cecum and cause bloody, mucoid stools and weight loss. They too pass eggs, but these eggs do not larvate—they are directly infective to another dog when eaten. And these eggs last in the soil for many years, so cleaning up stools is especially important. The adult worms have a thick portion that is an inch or two long, with a longer, whip-like tail. Their life cycle is about 12 weeks long. They cannot be killed by many of the routine wormers, such as pyrantel or Heartgard, but are normally treated with Panacur, Drontal, or Interceptor.

Tapeworms

Tapeworms are different from the other worms we have discussed in that they require an intermediate host to infect a dog. The adults pass eggs in packets which are consumed by the intermediate host, either a flea or a vermin such as a rat or mouse. The dog must then ingest either the flea or the vermin to be infected, and the worms grow to adults in the dog's small intestine. They attach to the wall to feed. The egg packets which pass from the anus or in the stool are actually segments dropped off the end of the worm. These segments look like rice grains when they are fresh, or like elongated sesame seeds when dried up, and are often seen in the hair under the tail. The worms themselves do not cause much damage, but the segments on the anus may cause itching, and people tend to object to finding the segments on their furniture and carpet. It takes about two to three weeks from ingestion before segments are passed, and they pass intermittently, not in every stool. Tapeworms are not killed by any of the heartworm preventives. Droncit, Drontal, and Cestex are the most commonly used wormers. Also, flea and/or vermin control are a necessary part of controlling reinfestation.

Coccidia

Coccidia are not actually worms, but they do infect the intestine of young pups. They are actually protozoans, like amoeba. They get inside the cells which line the small intestine, multiply, and cause the cells to burst, releasing more eggs. These eggs are passed in the stool and get into the environment where they are eaten by another dog. This disease is much worse in filthy conditions, and can only be cleaned out of a kennel by strict sanitation practices. Symptoms are mostly diarrhea, weight loss, and unthriftiness, but occasionally coccidia can spread to the brain and cause seizures in young pups. Treatment is a sulfa drug such as Albon or Bactrim, given for a minimum of five to seven days. Stool samples must be checked to be sure the eggs are gone, and sometimes treatment may be necessary for two weeks or more.

Giardia

Giardia is another protozoan parasite that infects the digestive tract of dogs, cats and humans, among other species. These organisms are passed in the stool of infected wildlife such as deer and raccoons, and feral dogs and cats, into streams, creeks and ponds. Other animals are then infected by drinking the water. Humans usually become infected by sampling "fresh mountain spring water." In a kennel setting, cysts that are passed in the stool are most likely transmitted to other dogs when the puppies are crowded and the humidity is high. Thus this disease is best controlled by keeping the kennel environment clean and dry and avoiding overcrowding. Besides drying out, the cysts can be killed by Roccal or a 1:16 bleach solution. The main symptom of giardiasis is watery diarrhea, along with weight loss. The disease can be treated with fenbendazole (Panacur) or metronidazole (Flagyl). There is also a new vaccine for Giardia that may be useful in reducing the disease incidence in infected kennels.

Winter Wolf Syndrome

Wolves, unlike most dogs, have only one estrus (heat) cycle per year. Pups are born during the spring months. During mating season, which occurs in the winter, hormonal levels rise. Along with an increased interest in mating, some wolves and wolfdogs display behavioral changes which include, in varying degrees, aggression toward other wolves and humans. This is known as Winter Wolf Syndrome. *WWS does not happen to all wolves or wolfdogs.* It is more commonly seen in pure wolves and high content wolfdogs, though it has been known to happen in some mid and lower content individuals.

WWS-type behavioral changes are more pronounced in unneutered males, due to the higher levels of testosterone. It can, however, occur in neutered males as well. Even females can display Winter Wolf Syndrome! But be careful; it is all too easy to attribute "crankiness" during winter months to Winter Wolf Syndrome. Wolfdogs, like people, can behave abberantly during any season, for any number of reasons. The cold weather in and of itself is stimulating and energizing, which could lead to behaviors which might be mistaken for WWS. And naturally, any canine who has not been well socialized, trained and desensitized to handling may display what could be interpreted as WWS. If you know your wolfdog is prone to behavioral changes during the winter months, make an extra effort to step up training, socialization and handling in the preceeding months.

A Learning Experience

To illustrate what dealing with true WWS is like, here is a first-hand account by Paul Ferrari, who became an expert on this phenomenon the hard way:

"The attack came the winter when Twoee was between three and four years old. I guess he matured that winter. Choctaw, Twoee's pen-mate, had been spayed in the middle of that January, before she came into season. One day in late January, I walked into the compound and he started to growl. I didn't think anything of it, but the next day I went in and walked to the top of the hill near the den they had dug and all hell broke loose. Eyes focused, hair up, tail up, he came right at me; a lot of noise, flashing teeth and claws. I will say he did not try to bite me—I think. I turned my back to him and covered my neck so he could not knock me down. I walked out of the compound with him on my back. The only damage I had was welts across my back and stomach. It looked like someone had beaten me with a whip. This also happened the next two days, only I stayed near the door. Monty Sloan from Wolf Park always said don't fight back, get out as calmly as possible, try not to let him get you on the ground and dominate you. If I would have fought back it would have escalated into an all-out attack. Monty also said, 'Forget your pride so you can play another day.'

If Two Feathers had gotten me down it's possible that he would have never let me in with him again. He really won, but he didn't know it. This behavior lasted until April. I found that if I carried the poop shovel and waved it in front of me he would stay away, but if I held it down, he would come to me to be petted. Even though he let me pet him, he still growled and showed teeth. I know if I didn't have the shovel he would have attacked again.

Winter Wolf Syndrome

I had daily contact with him throughout the whole winter in this manner. To get him back into the pen from the compound, treats, treats and more treats. My animals have never been hit; that is the quickest way to lose them. That April Twoee was neutered and Monty filmed it (that's another story). This all pertains to Winter Wolf Syndrome, moving up in rank against another pack member (me), protecting his female, and maturing. I have been in both male to male and female to female fights. The females are more deadly. They go for the kill. The males let me pull them apart and put one into the pen and lock the door. The females, on the other hand, fought for over an hour with me in the middle. Every time they got me they let go. Females are nasty! Neutering is the way to go. Twoee still gets a little snippy in the winter but that is to be expected.

TwoFeathers (pure wolf) with Choctaw, 80% wolf

Now that Twoee is eight years old, nine in May, his winters have gotten better each year since he has been neutered. This winter he has even been rolling over for me (on his own of course, I never push an animal). The last thing I would say is that I believe Winter Wolf Syndrome on a whole is captive-related, as this type of dominance would never last this long in the wild."

X Marks The Spot: Housebreaking

Okay, I'll admit it. Housebreaking is my least favorite part of bringing a new canine into the home. Let's face it, we all know housebreaking is no fun. Some new wolfdog owners, however, go so far as to ban their new fur-kids from ever being in the house, citing "impossible to housebreak" as the reason. While some wolfdogs, especially the higher contents, *can* present a major challenge when it comes to housebreaking, it can be done. With that in mind, here are some tips to make the process as quick and painless as possible.

Great Crates, Batman!

Crate training works on the principle that canines do not generally soil in their own area. In your home, a crate will become your wolfdog's "den," a place of security where he can sleep, hide out when he's feeling scared or sick, or go just to relax. Crate training also provides a safe way to transport your wolfdog, and is a good way to limit movement in one who is recovering from surgery or injury.

There are two basic types of crate. One is the metal fold-down type that looks like a cage. The other, which I prefer, is the heavy plastic snap-together type with metal grille door. Not only is the second type approved for airline transportation, but it provides more of an enclosed, safe-feeling space. If you do choose to use the fold-down kind, drape a towel or blanket over the top and sides to create more of a den effect.

A crate should be just big enough for your wolfdog to stand up and turn around in. If you've got a puppy, do not buy a huge crate for him to grow into. Having all that room will defeat the purpose.

241

You may need to buy a puppy-sized crate now and a larger one when he's bigger. Or, get a crate made by one of the companies who now include dividers so that you can shrink and then expand the puppy's space as needed.

The sooner you start crate training the better. Put a blanket or old sweatshirt with your scent on it in the bottom of the crate. This will not only make your wolfdog more comfortable, but will help the bonding process as well. Place the crate where you want him to sleep, i.e. by the side of your bed. When you first introduce the crate, be sure the door is propped open so as to not swing shut by accident. If your wolfdog doesn't go in to explore on his own, place a treat inside to entice him. You can even feed his meal in there. Make that crate a Doggie Disneyland, where wonderful things happen. Never force him in. If you do, the experience could create a lasting negative association with the crate and make things difficult for both of you. Be patient and let him explore this new place in his own time. It may help if you stand back from the crate and ignore it, rather than hovering nearby.

Each time your wolfdog goes into the crate, say, "In your house" in a high, pleasant voice. He will eventually come to associate this verbal cue with entering the crate. You can then use it later on to let him know when it's bedtime, or to load up for a crated car ride. After your wolfdog has become comfortable enough with the crate to explore it and perhaps eat a meal or two inside, practice briefly closing the door with him inside. Shut it for just a moment or two at first, then let him out. If he whines or barks when you close the door, ignore him. When he's quiet, let him out.

Once your wolfdog gets accustomed to being in the crate with the door closed, it's time to begin using it overnight. The first night say, "In your house," gently helping him in if necessary.

Close the door softly. You might want to put a favorite toy in with him. It is perfectly normal for any dog to whine, bark, or even throw tantrums the first night in a crate. Do *not* reward this behavior by petting, whispering soothing words, or worst of all, letting him out. Try simply ignoring him for a while. If that doesn't work, after a reasonable amount of time, simply tap the top of the crate gently

and say, "Quiet." Just don't get into the cycle of him whining and you saying "Quiet" each time, thereby reinforcing the behavior by responding to it at all. There are some dogs who will have trouble holding their urine all night (very young pups shouldn't be expected to), but you will come to know the difference between a normal whine and a need-to-urinate whine. If the whining becomes frantic during the night, open the crate door, pick your wolfdog up or snap a leash on and fast-walk him to the spot where you want him to eliminate. Do not let him wander out of the crate on his own, as he will most likely squat and urinate before making it to the proper area.

Each time your wolfdog prepares to eliminate (you'll quickly come to recognize that circle-and-sniff dance), repeat a phrase such as "Got to go potty?" in a soft, encouraging voice. This will become your verbal cue to signal him to do his business. Believe me, it comes in handy on rainy days or when you're in a rush! When he does, praise him in a soft, happy voice.

The Routine

First thing in the morning, open the crate door and carry or fast-walk your wolfdog to the proper elimination spot, using the verbal encouragement phrase and then lots of gentle praise as he goes. Once indoors again, refrain from letting him out of your sight, even briefly. Accidents happen in a split second; you need to be there to correct him *as* they happen, not later. Most canines learn quickly that we get this weird scary look on our faces when they eliminate in the house (some think it happens when they eliminate in front of us at all), so being the smart fur-kids they are, they begin to do it out of our sight. Prevent this by using baby gates to keep your fur-kid in the room with you, or by tying a long leash to your belt and attaching it to his collar. He should always be within your sight. That means not letting him get behind furniture or around corners. If you do catch him starting to squat, or to circle and sniff, startle him with a handclap or "Eh-eh!" and then quickly bring him to the proper spot. He may not go immediately. Be patient and give him a few moments. If he goes, praise! If not, try giving him a little exercise to stimulate elimination.

If you find an accident which has already happened, consider it your own mistake and clean it up quietly. No canine will associate a reprimand with the action that caused it, if the two happen more than 30 seconds apart. Some people, upon coming home and finding an "accident," drag their wolfdog to the spot and yell at him. They think their wolfdog understands this because of the way "he looks guilty." The truth is, he looks that way because he's being yelled at! He would have the same reaction if the person yelled at him that way with no incriminating "evidence" present. Wolfdogs whose owners do that learn to fear the return of their person, as their person often looks angry upon returning home!

For cleaning urine on carpets, be sure to use a product such as *Nature's Miracle*™ which removes the odor as well as the stain. This will discourage your wolfdog from urinating over the same spot again. Products which contain ammonia can actually stimulate canines to urinate where it is applied.

Take your wolfdog out to eliminate upon waking and after naps, after meals, after playtime and before bed. A very young pup may need to be taken out every one to two hours, day and night. A good rule of thumb is that a pup can hold it for as many hours as his age in months, plus one. In other words, a three month old pup should be able to hold it for four hours. It's important to go out with him so that you can give him the feedback that he's doing it in the right spot ("Good boy!"). If you must leave the house for a short period of time, or can't supervise, leave your wolfdog crated. Crating your wolfdog for short periods will not only prevent housebreaking accidents, but will also prevent unwanted chewing and destruction. Again, leave a favorite toy or bone in the crate with him. *Never leave a dog crated longer than four hours at a time, except overnight when you are there.*

Crate training will help immensely with housebreaking, but your vigilance in supervising your wolfdog's actions in the house is crucial. The more you're there to give well-timed information about proper and improper behavior, the faster he'll learn. Some canines become housebroken within seven to ten days, while others take a few weeks. Expect gradual improvement with some "accidents" along the way. Even after canines "get it," there will still be accidents now and then. This is normal. With time and patience, even those will become a thing of the past.

~ ~ ~ ~ ~ ~ ~ ~ ~ ~ ~ ~

Xtra Stuff!

...And now, just because it also starts with the letter X, here's some Xtra Stuff! (Okay, it doesn't really start with X, but the info is helpful and I wanted to squeeze it in, so there!)

Training Treats

For those of you who are concerned about your wolfdog gaining weight from training treats, or for those whose wolfdogs have food allergies:

Measure out 1/3 of your wolfdog's meal ration of kibble. Put it in a plastic bag along with some hot dogs or chicken, then seal and refrigerate overnight. In the morning, feed 2/3 of his usual kibble ration. Throughout the day, use the bagged kibble (minus the hot dogs/chicken) as training treats. The kibble will have absorbed the yummy food odors and are now Yummy Training Treats!

Gentle Mouth

Many wolfdogs have a problem taking treats gently. Or I should say, *we* have a problem when they don't, as we have a certain fondness for our fingers. One way to remedy the situation, for those whose wolfdogs are not *too* rough with their mouths, is to feed kibble by hand, a piece at a time. If the wolfdog takes it too roughly, say "Eh-eh" sharply, then present it again, saying "Gentle" in a low, soothing voice. Most canines learn pretty quickly how to earn that piece of kibble.

For wolfdogs who are just too rough to attempt hand-feeding, try this trick: Place a treat on a metal spoon and present it to your wolfdog. One chomp on metal is enough to convince most wolfdogs that biting down hard is *not* a good thing. As he takes the treat gently, softly say, "Gentle." Once he's gotten the idea, intersperse taking the treat from the spoon with taking the treat from your hand. For example, two treats from the spoon, one from your hand. It's more likely he'll take it gently from your hands once he's already in "gentle mode."

Another trick for super-rough chompers is to get some metal finger splints from a medical supply store. Put them on the fingers you feed food with, and let Timber have a go at it. Like the spoon, the metal is a deterrent to chomping too roughly. Pair the taking of treats gently with the cue "Gentle" as above.

Turn the page for some more Xtra Stuff...

Wolfdogs A-Z

Carsickness

"My wolfdog gets carsick" is a common complaint, especially among puppy owners. Most pups outgrow carsickness, but it is most unpleasant for pup and owner alike in the meantime. Here are a few solutions:

- Don't feed your pup for two hours before car rides; withhold water for the last hour.
- Get your pup used to car trips in short increments. Go around the block and come back.
- Keep windows rolled down as much as safety will allow.
- Ask your veterinarian about using over-the-counter products such as Dramamine. Get his okay and the correct dosage for your pup's body weight.
- Many people have reported success using ginger root for their carsick canines. Inquire at a health food store about this natural herbal remedy.
- There are homeopathic remedies specifically for carsickness. Ask your practitioner of homeopathic medicine which would be appropriate for your wolfdog.
- Anti-static strips. I mention this one, although it sounds odd, because there is a lot of anecdotal evidence that it works. The theory is that canines become carsick due to the buildup of static electricity in the vehicle. Anti-static strips, placed on the car's bumper (or somewhere in the car away from the woofer), remove the charge from the air. Hey, it's worth a try and can't hurt. The strips can be found through car product dealers.
- If your wolfdog is riding free in the back seat, crate him. This may provide a smoother ride, resulting in less carsickness. Do not let him ride on the floor of the passenger seat, where there is a high rate of vibration.

Bottlefeeding

*While I do not advocate breeding your wolfdog, if you already
have a pup, you may find this section useful. While some wolfdog
owners strongly believe in bottlefeeding, others do not. Get all
the information you can, and make the right decision for your
own wolfdog.*

*The following information was contributed by Gudrun Dunn and
Christine Burkett.*

Gudrun Dunn:

"While not all wolfdog pups need to be pulled from their mothers
before natural weaning, bottlefeeding uppermid to high content
litters is extremely important. The earlier pups are socialized to
humans, the better. However, there is absolutely no benefit to
bottlefeeding mid/lowermid to low content litters. The benefits
of leaving them with momma are great, and their overall
socialization will not lack for it if they otherwise receive proper
care and handling.

The wrong way to bottlefeed a pup is to shove a nipple in their
mouth periodically. The correct way is to nurture—make contact
with the pup, hold it close, treat each as an individual being,
massage the pup's tummy, talk to it gently—get the pup used to
its human caretakers.

I've used Christine Burkett's "Casa Lobo Kennels Bottlefeeding
Formula" with great success, and feel that it is much better than
any commercial product. The beauty of this formula is that you
can adapt it to suit the needs of your growing pup."

Casa Lobo Kennels' Bottlefeeding Recipe

Christine Burkett: "This is written for an entire litter, the amount designed to feed four to six pups. After the first few days, I am mixing a new batch every 18 hours or so.

I have always pulled at ten days and have yet to experience any real problems by doing so. Below is the formula that several vets have approved. It is very similar to the one used by Wolf Park.

Either: 1 can goat's milk (one can = 13 oz.),
    and 13 oz. water *or* Gatorade *or* Pedialyte
  or 26 oz. fresh goat's milk;
      3 heaping Tbsp. Dannon plain yogurt (I recommend
      Dannon for the enzymes);
      1 Tbsp. white corn syrup;
      1 teaspoon Knox gelatin dissolved in hot water;
      1 jar beef baby food (be sure there is
      no onion powder in it); and
      1 Tbsp. Canine Red Cell or appropriate
      amount of baby vitamin drops.

Put this all in a blender and blend well. Note: If using fresh goat's milk, you wouldn't add the water, etc. but would need 26 oz. of fresh milk.

Depending on when you pull the pups and start them on formula, don't be alarmed if they don't take but a small amount. It usually takes a few hours for them to even show any interest in a bottle. I have had some go as long as 12-18 hours before I could get even an ounce into them. Just keep at it and be patient with them. They will come around but don't overfeed them too early. This can cause problems. Start with an ounce every couple of hours for a day or two, then move them up to an ounce and half, etc. At about three weeks I start adding a bit of baby rice cereal and start adding whole buttermilk (start backing off on the goats milk, water and yogurt) and start using an Infa-feeder (infant formula bottle, larger nipple hole) as I thicken the formula with cereal.

I might vary by a day or two on starting the rice and then adding a high protein, meat-based kibble (depends on the voraciousness of the appetite) but that's basically what I do. It is very important to run the moistened kibble through the blender thoroughly. It needs to be completely softened and blended well, or it will stop the Infa-feeder up. In the meantime, the pup is getting desperate and you and he both will wind up with gruel all over yourselves.

From this age onward (three and a half to four weeks), instead of kibble you can start adding very finely minced raw meats in small amounts and put it into the Infa-feeder with the formula. I would wait until I had moved them on to the pan to add the meat but if it can be ground finely enough to go through the holes in the Infa-feeder, that will work too."

You Know Your Wolfdogs Have Taken Over Your Life When...

(If you've got wolfdogs, you'd best have a
sense of humor. Relax and enjoy!)

1. There's no room for ice cream in your freezer, thanks to the 40 lbs.of chicken backs.

2. Home Depot has become your shopping hot spot.

3. When looking for a place to live, the size of the house is secondary to the size of the yard.

4. You wake up one day and notice that all your close friends are also "wolf nuts" who are just as crazy as you are.

5. Your garage has become a storage facility for chain link, hog wire and rebar.

6. You catch your spouse watching you worriedly as you jump for joy over a firm stool sample.

7. You go house hunting, but lust after and buy the chain-link dog run panels that are lying around instead.

8. You toss and turn in your sleep, chanting "I *am* the alpha, I *am* the alpha..."

9. The phrase "How are the kids?" does not refer to two-leggeds.

10. You've discovered that your home, once thought to be your castle, is actually one large den... and you wouldn't have it any other way.

Zees Ees Zee End

Well friends, this is the end. Or, in compliance with the letter Z, see above. I hope you enjoyed this book and found some of the ideas and information helpful for you and your four-footed friends. Please refer to the *Resource* chapter for some wonderful books, videos and other ways to continue your pursuit of knowledge in canine training and behavior.

Have fun training, and don't forget to the most important thing... lots of love and tummyrubs!

Phantom Publishing

www.phantompub.com

Stay tuned!